ROADMAPS
FOR DAILY
WORSHIP

[100 DAYS OF PRAISE]

ROADMAPS FOR DAILY WORSHIP

[100 DAYS OF PRAISE]

JIM ALTIZER

SOUND & LIGHT PUBLISHING

THOUSAND OAKS, CALIFORNIA

COPYRIGHT ©2000 BY SOUND & LIGHT PUBLISHING

Library of Congress Card #00-190742

First published in the year 2000 by
Sound & Light Publishing
1534 N. Moorpark Road, Suite #109
Thousand Oaks, CA 91360
805-496-9664

ISBN: 0-615-11437-7

Scripture taken from the *Holy Bible, New International Version.*
Copyright © 1973, 1978, 1984, International Bible Society.
Used by permission of Zondervan Bible Publishers.

Scripture taken from the *Holy Bible, New American Standard
Version.* Copyright © 1960, 1962, 1963, 1968, 1971, 1972,
1973, 1975, 1977, The Lockman Foundation. Used by permission of Thomas Nelson Publishers.

The Practice of the Presence of God, by Brother Lawrence
Adapted, Categorized, Personalized by Jim Altizer, from the title
The Practice of the Presence of God, published by Fleming H. Revell
Company, 1958. LOC#58-10027

ABOUT THE AUTHOR
Jim Altizer is a professional trumpet player who has also worked
as a part-time worship leader for the last 20 years. He is married
and has four children. Jim and his wife Mary Kay tour nationally
as the duo "Ivory & Brass."

Printed in the United States of America

To the Men who made me one
Leland W. Altizer
Gerry Alden
Don Schmierer
Fred Jantz

And to my wife
Mary Kay

And my children
Morgan
Nicole
Jeff
Taylor

Contents

Contents

Introduction

Becoming *religious* is a simple process: join the club, learn the secret handshake, master the vernacular, memorize the rituals. Presto—you're religious! Worship, in this context, is merely a hoop to jump through that shows you belong. If by contrast Christianity is described as a personal *relationship* with God, rather than a religion, then one is left both awe-struck and wondering: awe-struck that creature and Creator, flesh and Spirit, seen and Unseen, could commune on such a level as to be termed a relationship; wonder regarding what to say, think, feel, and do; wonder regarding what it is to worship in the context of a *relationship*, and how to do it appropriately.[1]

God has left a well-lit path into His presence. Psalm 119 says *Thy Word is a lamp unto my feet and a light unto my path.* The Bible is full of instruction on how to enter into His presence. All we need to do is to walk the path with our whole heart, mind, soul, and strength.

Any relationship has its ups and downs. If you get tongue-tied, dispassionate, uncreative, or uninspired, there are resources in the back of the book to use. If we persevere, we will find ourselves in relationship with the King of the universe, and we will see Him respond in a marvelous way:

"He will take great delight in you,
he will quiet you with his love,
he will rejoice over you with singing."
(Zephaniah 3:17)

---

[1] Jim Altizer, *Worship; Religion Or Relationship. Ten Essays On Worship,* (Sound & Light Publishing, 1992), p. 13.

DEVOTIONALS

PSALMS

Psalm 5 🌿

PRAY

Verses 1–3: Give ear to my words, O Lord, consider my meditation, hearken unto the voice of my cry, my King and my God, for unto Thee do I pray. My voice wilt thou hear in the morning, O Lord. In the morning will I direct my prayer unto Thee and will look up.

Pray silently to the Lord… Cast your cares upon Him…

CONFESS

Verses 4–6: You are not a God who takes pleasure in evil; with You the wicked cannot dwell. The arrogant cannot stand in your presence; you hate all who do wrong. You destroy those who tell lies; bloodthirsty and deceitful men the Lord abhors.

Confess aloud: "Lord, I *am* sometimes deceitful; I have done wrong; and I am arrogant. Forgive me, for I want to stand in Your presence."

WORSHIP

Verses 7–8: But I, by your great mercy, will come into your house; in reverence will I bow down toward your holy temple. Lead me, O Lord, in your righteousness.

Think: "Lord, I come, not because I am good, but because of Your mercy. I come in reverence. I lay myself low before You."

REJOICE

Verses 11–12: But let all who take refuge in you be glad; let them ever sing for joy. Spread your protection over them, that those who love your name may rejoice in you. For surely, O Lord, you bless the righteous; you surround them with your favor as with a shield.

Sing: "Praise the Name of Jesus"

✤ Psalm 8

MAJESTIC

Verse 1a: O Lord, our Lord, how majestic is your name in all the earth!

Worshiper of God, bow yourself to acknowledge his majesty, while you say, "I bow in your presence, O Most High!"

GLORIOUS

Verse 1b: You have set your glory above the heavens.

Think of it! The glory of God is more spectacular than the clearest starry night ever seen. A voice adds nothing to His glory, but a worshipping heart pleases Him! Set your heart to honor His glory.

CREATOR

Verse 3: I consider your heavens, the work of your fingers, the moon and the stars, which you have put in place.

Take a moment to consider the *vastness* and the *variety* of His creation, and then try to speak words of praise mixed with amazement.

LOVING

Verses 4–6: What is man that you are mindful of him, the son of man that you care for him? You made him a little lower than the heavenly beings and crowned him with glory and honor. You made him ruler over the works of your hands; you put everything under his feet.

Think on His love for you personally. Think of how He has honored you. Think of how He has trusted you with His creation. Thank Him, and pray for wisdom to live up to his trust.

Psalm 19 ❧

GOD IN HIS CREATION
Verse 1: The heavens declare the glory of God; the skies proclaim the work of his hands.

Think on the beauty of creation. Consider the variety and intricacy, and consciously give God credit for it.

Meditate on the words of "How Great Thou Art."

GOD IN HIS WORD
Verses 7–8: The law of the Lord is perfect, reviving the soul. The statutes of the Lord are trustworthy, making wise the simple. The precepts of the Lord are right, giving joy to the heart. The commands of the Lord are radiant, giving light to the eyes.

List promises from God's Word that you may know.

GOD IN OUR HEARTS
Verses 12–13: Who can discern his errors? Forgive my hidden faults. Keep your servant also from willful sins; may they not rule over me.

Take time now to listen to God, and to allow Him to put His finger on any "hidden fault" or upon any "willful sin" in your life. Acknowledge His Lordship and His forgiveness in this area of your life.

GOD IN OUR WORSHIP
Verse 14: May the words of my mouth and the meditations of my heart be pleasing in your sight, O Lord, my Rock and my Redeemer.

Pick four times throughout the day to pray this verse, and then do it.

❦ Psalm 24

CREATOR

Verses 1–2: The earth is the Lord's and everything in it, the world, and all who live in it; for he founded it upon the seas and established it upon the waters.

Speak some words of admiration to the Creator; acknowledge His hand in everything you see.

HOLY

Verses 3–4: Who may ascend the hill of the Lord? Who may stand in his holy place? He who has clean hands and a pure heart, who does not lift up his soul to an idol or swear by what is false.

"Lord, as I stand in your holy place, I notice that my hands are stained with my many sins. My heart is stained with impure motivations. I have worshiped at the idols of materialism, and have not always told the whole truth. Forgive me, Lord."

KING

Verses 7–10: Lift up your heads, O you gates; be lifted up, you ancient doors, that the King of glory may come in. Who is this King of glory? The Lord strong and mighty, the Lord mighty in battle. Lift up your heads, O you gates; lift them up, you ancient doors, that the King of glory may come in. Who is he, this King of glory? The Lord Almighty—he is the King of glory.

"Come into me, Lord. I open my heart to You. Come into me, Lord. I open my spirit to You. Come into me, Lord. I open my mind to You. Come into me, Lord. I give you complete control. You are the King of glory."

Psalm 27 ❦

TRUST IN HIM

Verses 1, 3: The Lord is my light and my salvation—whom shall I fear? The Lord is the stronghold of my life—of whom shall I be afraid? Though an army besiege me, my heart will not fear; though war break out against me, even then will I be confident.

Say out loud: "Lord, I trust in You rather than in my_____."

abilities	education	possessions
reputation	savings	intellect
ambitions	talents	stamina

WORSHIP HIM

Verse 4: One thing I ask of the Lord, this is what I seek: that I may dwell in the house of the Lord all the days of my life, to gaze upon the beauty of the Lord and to seek him in his temple.

Quietly acknowledge his presence; gaze upon his beauty; recite his attributes; seek his face.

ASK HIM

Verse 7: Hear my voice when I call, O Lord; be merciful to me and answer me.

Ask the Lord to intervene in your "out of control" areas.

HOPE IN HIM

Verses 13–14: I am still confident of this: I will see the goodness of the Lord in the land of the living. Wait for the Lord; be strong and take heart and wait for the Lord.

"Lord, today when I have opportunities to hope in circumstances, I'm going to choose instead to hope in your goodness. I wait on You, Lord. Make me strong of heart as I choose You over everything else."

❦ Psalm 33

Rejoice In Him

Verses 1–3: Sing joyfully to the Lord, you righteous; it is fitting for the upright to praise him. Praise the Lord with the harp; make music to him on the ten-stringed lyre. Sing to him a new song; play skillfully, and shout for joy.

Read in a loud voice: "Your salvation is better than finding the cure to cancer. Your forgiveness feels like the weight of the world is lifted from my heart. Your provision calms the deepest fears of my soul. Your guarantee of heaven is the hope of my life."

Lean On Him

Verses 4–5: For the word of the Lord is right and true; he is faithful in all he does. The Lord loves righteousness and justice; the earth is full of his unfailing love.

Meditate on these words: Right; True; Faithful; Righteous; Just; Unfailing. Decide to lean on Him above all else!

Trust In Him

Verse 11: The plans of the Lord stand firm forever, the purposes of his heart through all generations.

Where is your trust is today? Is it in bank accounts, or abilities, or jobs, or the economy? Silently place your trust in Him.

Hope In Him

Verses 20, 22: We wait in hope for the Lord; he is our help and our shield. May your unfailing love rest upon us, O Lord, ever as we put our hope in you.

Speaking out loud, personalize this prayer. "I wait.…You are my help… my shield… I put my hope…"

Psalm 34 ❧

EXALT THE LORD

Verses 1–3: I will bless the Lord at all times; his praise will always be on my lips. My soul will boast in the Lord; let the afflicted hear and rejoice. Glorify the Lord with me; let us *exalt* his name together.

"Lord, Your name is higher than _____; more powerful than _____; holier than _____."

PRAISE THE LORD

Verses 4–6: I sought the Lord, and he answered me; he delivered me from all my fears. Those who look to him are radiant; their faces are never covered with shame. This poor man called, and the Lord heard him, and he saved him out of all his troubles.

Those who tasted the world and came up empty should praise Him for deliverance. Those who came to Christ early in life should praise Him for being spared from the world's emptiness.

FEAR THE LORD

Verses 7–9: The angel of the Lord encamps around those who fear him, and he delivers them. Taste and see that the Lord is good; blessed is the man who takes refuge in him. Fear the Lord, you his saints, for those who fear him lack nothing.

Fear the Lord! Fear Him, but do not be afraid of Him. "Dear Lord, I fear displeasing You; I fear misunderstanding You; I fear disobeying You; I fear dishonoring You; I fear misrepresenting You; I fear loving You half-heartedly; I fear missing Your plan. I fear You, but I am not afraid of You. Rather, I praise you."

# Psalm 40

Recount His Works

Verses 1–3: I waited patiently for the Lord; he turned to me and heard my cry. He lifted me out of the slimy pit, out of the mud and mire; he set my feet on a rock and gave me a firm place to stand. He put a new song in my mouth, a hymn of praise to our God. Many will see and fear and put their trust in the Lord.

Take this opportunity to recount the changes God has brought to your life. Silently list the workings of God in your life.

Trust In Him

Verses 4–5: Blessed is the man who makes the Lord his trust, who does not look to the proud, to those who turn aside to false gods. Many, O Lord my God, are the wonders you have done. The things you planned for us no one can recount to you; were I to speak and tell of them, they would be too many to declare.

Take time to place your trust in God. If it helps, picture one hand holding the many things you depend on: work; relationships; health; savings accounts; abilities; etc. Now place all your hope in the hand of Almighty God.

Speak Of Him

Verses 9–10: I proclaim righteousness in the great assembly; I do not seal my lips, as you know, O Lord. I do not hide your righteousness in my heart; I speak of your faithfulness and salvation. I do not conceal your love and your truth from the great assembly.

Speak aloud of His faithfulness by completing this phrase: "God, You are _____." (great; mighty; creative; etc.)

"Dear Lord, please give me the opportunity today to tell someone of your faithfulness and salvation."

Psalm 51 ❦

Worship through the prayer of a man who committed adultery and premeditated murder. Psalm 51 was written by King David after Nathan the Prophet convicted him of his sin. David crawled back to God, eventually to be called "a man after God's own heart."

REPENT
Verses 1–3: Have mercy on me, O God, according to your unfailing love; according to your great compassion blot out my transgressions. Wash away all my iniquity and cleanse me from my sin. For I know my transgressions, and my sin is always before me.

Take a moment to silently acknowledge anything in your life which would keep *you* from God.

RECEIVE
Verses 7–9: Cleanse me with hyssop, and I will be clean; wash me, and I will be whiter than snow. Let me hear joy and gladness; let the bones you have crushed rejoice. Hide your face from my sins and blot out all my iniquity.

Say this out loud, three times. "Lord, I accept Your forgiveness—and by Your strength—will forgive myself."

REACH
Verses 10–12: Create in me a pure heart, O God, and renew a steadfast spirit within me. Do not cast me from your presence or take your Holy Spirit from me. Restore to me the joy of your salvation and grant me a willing spirit, to sustain me.

What is it that you would have God do in your life? Silently ask God to do a work in you. Give thanks like a person who has been brought from death to life.

 # Psalm 61

Outline by Jamie Lay and Jim Altizer

LAMENT

Verses 1–2: Hear my cry, O God; listen to my prayer. From the ends of the earth I call to you, I call as my heart grows faint; lead me to the rock that is higher than I.

Picture yourself bowing before God. Pray these verses to Him, picturing Him listening intently to you.

REFUGE

Verses 3–4: For you have been my refuge, a strong tower against the foe. I long to dwell in your tent forever and take refuge in the shelter of your wings.

Imagine God as a tent. Crawl into Him. Breathe a sigh of relief that He is surrounding you; He is protecting you; He is sheltering you. Give Him thanks for these mercies.

PETITION

Verses 5–7: For you have heard my vows, O God; you have given me the heritage of those who fear your name. Increase the days of the king's life, his years for many generations. May he be enthroned in God's presence forever; Appoint your love and faithfulness to protect him.

Pray these verses for the president, whether you agree with him or not. Also for your governor; mayor; boss; spouse.

PRAISE

Verse 8: Then will I ever sing praise to your name and fulfill my vows day after day.

Speak His names. Sing or speak "Praise the Name of Jesus."

Psalm 63 ❦

Earnestly Seek God

Verse 1: O God, you are my God, earnestly I seek you; my soul thirsts for you, my body longs for you, in a dry and weary land where there is no water.

Whisper this prayer to God.

Earnestly Praise God

Verses 2–4: I have seen you in the sanctuary and beheld your power and your glory. Because your love is better than life, my lips will glorify you. I will praise you as long as I live, and in your name I will lift up my hands.

Think on the power and glory of God. Do you think His love is better than life? Confess as sin whatever you treat as better than His love. In obedience to his word, lift your hands and speak words of praise to God.

Earnestly Thank God

Verses 5–8: My soul will be satisfied as with the richest of foods; with singing lips my mouth will praise you. On my bed I remember you; I think of you through the watches of the night. Because you are my help, I sing in the shadow of your wing. My soul clings to you; your right hand upholds me.

Picture your soul grabbing onto His feet. Picture His hand holding you up. Give Him thanks for his goodness. Place something on your pillow right now to remind you to go to sleep thinking of and praising God.

# Psalm 86

Outline by Jamie Lay

SUPPLICATION
Verses 1–6: Hear, O Lord, and answer me, for I am poor and needy.

Guard my life, for I am devoted to you. You are my God; save your servant who trusts in you. Have mercy on me, O Lord, for I call to you all day long. Bring joy to your servant, for to you, O Lord, I lift up my soul. You are forgiving and good, O Lord, abounding in love to all who call to you. Hear my prayer, O Lord;

God is listening intently! Speak your requests to Him.

RECOGNIZE GOD'S POSITION
Verses 9–10: All the nations you have made will come and worship before you, O Lord; they will bring glory to your name. For you are great and do marvelous deeds; you alone are God.

Recount God's deeds, both in history, and in your life.

RECOGNIZE GOD'S AUTHORITY
Verses 11–12: Teach me your way, O Lord, and I will walk in your truth; give me an undivided heart, that I may fear your name. I will praise you, O Lord my God with all my heart; I will glorify your name forever.

Pray verse 11 slowly and thoughtfully. Do verse 12.

RECOGNIZE GOD'S POWER
Verses 15–16: You, O Lord, are a compassionate and gracious God, slow to anger, abounding in love and faithfulness. Turn to me and have mercy on me; grant your strength to your servant and save the son of your maidservant.

Ask God to give you his strength. Thank him for his compassion, grace, patience, love, and faithfulness.

Psalm 90 ❦

God Is Self-Existent

Verses 1–2: Lord, you have been our dwelling place throughout all generations. Before the mountains were born or you brought forth the earth and the world, from everlasting to everlasting you are God.

"Dear God, I acknowledge but do not understand that You had no origin. You are the cause of everything, but were caused by nothing. Accept my worship."

God Is Eternal

Verses 3–4: You turn men back to dust, saying, "Return to dust, O sons of men." For a thousand years in your sight are like a day that has just gone by, or like a watch in the night.

"Dear God, to You, everything that will happen has already happened. You appear at the beginning and at the end of time simultaneously. Hallelujah!"

I Am Transient

Verses 8–10: You have set our iniquities before you, our secret sins in the light of your presence. The length of our days is seventy years, or eighty, if we have the strength.

"Dear Lord! Knowing that my secret sins are in the light of Your presence undoes me! You are my only hope."

God Is Merciful

Verses 14: Satisfy us in the morning with your unfailing love, that we may sing for joy and be glad all our days. May the favor of the Lord our God rest upon us.

"Dear God, I am here because You, in your mercy and goodness, have confronted my suffering and guilt. Hallelujah, what a savior!"

❦ Psalm 91

He Shelters Us

Verses 1–2: He who dwells in the shelter of the Most High will rest in the shadow of the Almighty. I will say of the Lord, "He is my refuge and my fortress, my God in whom I trust."

"God, again today I say that You are my refuge; You are my fortress. I trust only in You."

He Delivers Us

Verses 5–8: You will not fear the terror of night, nor the arrow that flies by day, nor the pestilence that stalks in the darkness, nor the plague that destroys at midday. A thousand may fall at your side, ten thousand at your right hand, but it will not come near you.

"Lord, I often demand an explanation when things go wrong, but rarely notice the many times You have delivered me from temptation and danger. I give you thanks for the countless unseen times You have delivered me from who-knows-what."

He Saves Us

Verses 14–16: "Because he loves me" says the Lord, "I will protect him, for he acknowledges my name. He will call upon me, and I will answer him; I will be with him in trouble, I will deliver him and honor him. With long life will I satisfy him and show him my salvation."

Meditate on how life would be without Christ. Thank him for saving you from hopelessness. Remember the freedom that is yours in Christ.

Psalm 95 🌱

Outline by Ronald Allen

COME IN JOY!

Verses 1–5: Come, let us sing for joy to the Lord; let us shout aloud to the Rock of our salvation. Let us come before him with thanksgiving and extol him with music and song. For the Lord is the great God, the great King above all gods. In his hand are the depths of the earth, and the mountain peaks belong to him. The sea is his, for he made it, and his hands formed the dry land.

Get to an "alone" place. In a very loud voice, personalize these verses as your praise to God.

COME IN REVERENCE

Verses 6–7: Come, let us bow down in worship, let us kneel before the Lord our Maker; for he is our God and we are the people of his pasture, the flock under his care.

In that same "alone" place, kneel. Speaking reverently, personalize these verses as your offering to the Lord.

COME IN FAITH

Verses 8–9: Do not harden your hearts as you did at Meribah, as you did that day at Massah in the desert, where your fathers tested and tried me, though they had seen what I did.

"Lord, show me where I have hardened my heart. Bring your amazing works to my mind again, that my faith might ignite. I believe in You, Lord."

❧ Psalm 99

He Is Above All

Verses 1–3: The Lord reigns, let the nations tremble; he sits enthroned between the cherubim, let the earth shake. Great is the Lord in Zion; he is exalted over all the nations. Let them praise your great and awesome name—he is holy.

Think of three new combinations that praise his "great and awesome name," i.e. Ageless and Eternal One; Mighty and Everlasting Shepherd.

He Is Just And Righteous

Verses 4–5: The King is mighty, he loves justice—you have established equity; in Jacob you have done what is just and right. Exalt the Lord our God and worship at his footstool; he is holy.

Thank God for receiving what you did not deserve (grace). Exalt God for not giving you what you did deserve (judgment).

He Is Forgiving

Verses 7–9: He spoke to them from the pillar of cloud; they kept his statutes and the decrees he gave them. O Lord our God, you answered them; you were to Israel a forgiving God, though you punished their misdeeds.

What is one statute or decree you are not obeying? Let the Holy Spirit bring to mind an area you need to confess.

He Is To Be Worshiped

Verse 9: Exalt the Lord our God and worship at his holy mountain, for the Lord our God is holy.

Speak words of reverence and awe to the Lord. Bow before Him.

Psalm 100 🌱

GIVE HIM PRAISE
Verses 1–2: Shout for joy to the Lord, all the earth. Worship the Lord with gladness; come before him with joyful songs.

Speak some words of praise to the Lord; end by shouting the word "hallelujah."

ACKNOWLEDGE HIS SOVEREIGNTY
Verse 3: Know that the Lord is God. It is he who made us, and we are his; we are his people, the sheep of his pasture.

"Lord, I ascribe to You your rightful place in my life. I give You access to every area of my being, and I put my trust in you to lead, protect, and provide for me."

GIVE HIM THANKS
Verse 4: Enter his gates with thanksgiving and his courts with praise; give thanks to him and praise his name. For the Lord is good and his love endures forever; his faithfulness continues through all generations.

Take some silent moments to thank and praise God for both the ordinary and for the extraordinary things He has done. Think on his goodness. Think on his never-ending love. Think on his faithfulness. Give him thanks.

❦ Psalm 103

His Blessings

Verses 1–5: Praise the Lord, O my soul; all my inmost being, praise his holy name. Praise the Lord, O my soul, and forget not all his benefits—who forgives all your sins and heals all your diseases, who redeems your life from the pit and crowns you with love and compassion, who satisfies your desires with good things so that your youth is renewed like the eagle's.

Speak his blessings: "He forgives; He heals; He redeems; He crowns me with love; He satisfies; He renews."

His Character

Verses 6–10: The Lord works righteousness and justice for all the oppressed. He made known his ways to Moses, his deeds to the people of Israel: The Lord is compassionate and gracious, slow to anger, abounding in love. He will not always accuse, nor will he harbor his anger forever; he does not treat us as our sins deserve or repay us according to our iniquities.

Speak his attributes: "You are compassionate.…You are gracious.…You are slow to anger.…You abound in love.…You won't stay mad.…You forgive.…Your love for me is endless."

His Heart

Verses 11–13: For as high as the heavens are above the earth, so great is his love for those who fear him; as far as the east is from the west, so far has he removed our transgressions from us. As a father has compassion on his children, so the Lord has compassion on those who fear him.

Speak the results of His love: "His love for me is great; He has removed my sin; He has had compassion on me; He knows and loves me completely; He gives me His righteousness."

Psalm 105 ❦

Give Thanks
Verse 1: Give thanks to the Lord, call on his name; make known among the nations what he has done.

To God; out loud: "Thank you for _____."

(3 things)

Sing
Verse 2: Sing to him, sing praise to him; tell of all his wonderful acts.

Sing your favorite hymn or chorus softly to God.

Glory In His Name
Verse 3: Glory in his holy name; let the hearts of those who seek the Lord rejoice.

Go through the alphabet and try to speak a name or attribute of God for each letter. Use the appendices if you need help.

Look To The Lord
Verse 4: Look to the Lord and his strength; seek his face always.

Is there one area of life in which are you working in your own strength? Decide to depend upon God rather than trusting in yourself.

Remember
Verse 5: Remember the wonders he has done, his miracles, and the judgments he pronounced.

Recount again what God has done in you that you could not have done in yourself.

❦ Psalm 113

GOD'S COMMAND TO PRAISE

Verses 1–3: Praise the Lord. Praise, O servants of the Lord, praise the name of the Lord. Let the name of the Lord be praised, both now and forever more. From the rising of the sun to the place where it sets, the name of the Lord is to be praised.

"Lord, I understand your command for servants of God to praise your *name,* both now and forever. I give myself to obey this command. I praise your holy name today, and will praise You for the rest of my life."

GOD'S REASON TO PRAISE

Verses 4–6: The Lord is exalted over all the nations, his glory above the heavens. Who is like the Lord our God, the One who sits enthroned on high, who stoops down to look on the heavens and the earth?

God does not owe his creation an explanation for his commands, but He gives a reason to praise anyway. Speak out loud of the incomparable nature of God. "There is no one like my God; He is totally *other* than any being in the entire universe. Praise Him!"

GOD'S LEGACY TO US

Verses 7–9: He raises the poor from the dust and lifts the needy from the ash heap; he seats them with princes, with the princes of their people. He settles the barren woman in her home as a happy mother of children. Praise the Lord.

God is in the business of life-change! We were lost and have been found. He has brought life where there once was decay. He has given hope in place of hopelessness. This is called grace, and it is amazing! Sing or speak the words to "Amazing Grace."

Psalm 118 ❦

His Love Endures Forever
Verses 1–4: Give thanks to the Lord, for he is good; his love endures forever. Let Israel say: "His love endures forever." Let the house of Aaron say: "His love endures forever." Let those who fear the Lord say: "His love endures forever."

Read again, out loud.

He Is Our Refuge
Verses 5–9: In my anguish I cried to the Lord, and he answered by setting me free. The Lord is with me; I will not be afraid. What can man do to me? The Lord is with me; he is my helper. I will look in triumph on my enemies. It is better to take refuge in the Lord than to trust in man. It is better to take refuge in the Lord than to trust in princes.

Give silent thanks for the refuge you have found in the Lord.

He Is Our Righteousness
Verses 19–21: Open for me the gates of righteousness; I will enter and give thanks to the Lord. This is the gate of the Lord through which the righteous may enter. I will give you thanks, for you answered me; you have become my salvation.

Stop and give true thanks for your salvation.

He Is Our Cornerstone
Verses 22–23: The stone the builders rejected has become the capstone; the Lord has done this, and it is marvelous in our eyes.

"Lord, today I set my life on your firm foundation, and speak your Word as my psalm of praise (verses 28). You are my God, and I will give you thanks; you are my God, and I will Exalt you."

❧ Psalm 121

GOD IS STRONG

Verses 1–2: I lift up my eyes to the hills—where does my help come from? My help comes from the Lord, the Maker of heaven and earth.

"Lord, it makes sense to ask earth's Maker for help, but I confess I still seek help from the helpless and hope from the hopeless. I decide again today to seek *your* strength."

GOD IS VIGILANT

Verses 3–4 : He will not let your foot slip—he who watches over you will not slumber; indeed, he who watches over Israel will neither slumber nor sleep.

Silently consider the constant and vigilant watch-care of God Almighty.

GOD IS A SHELTER

Verses 5–6: The Lord watches over you—the Lord is your shade at your right hand; the sun will not harm you by day, nor the moon by night.

Resolve to rest under his protection. Resolve to credit Him for any good fortune you might have experienced from His protection.

GOD IS A GUARDIAN

Verses 7–8: The Lord will keep you from all harm—He will watch over your life; the Lord will watch over your coming and going both now and forevermore.

"Lord, go before me today. Clear the path for me to obey You. Work your plan in my life today. Guard me, not just from danger, but also from temptation. Protect me from myself. I put my trust in You."

Handwritten margin notes: Father I want you to hold me • Everlasting God • Still

Psalm 136 ❦

Outline by Jamie Lay

EXALTATION

Verses 1–3: Give thanks to the Lord, for he is good. His love endures forever. Give thanks to the God of gods. His love endures forever. Give thanks to the Lord of lords. His love endures forever.

With a pen, write HLEF on your hand. Every time you notice it, let it remind you to say His love endures forever.

REVERENCE

Verses 4–5: To him who alone does great wonders, His love endures forever. Who by his understanding made the heavens, His love endures forever.

Think on the vast amount of knowledge and understanding that God effortlessly has. Think on the great wonders He has performed. Picture Him sitting above the created worlds. Bow yourself at the waist and speak words of adoration.

DELIVERANCE

Verses 10–12: To him who struck down the firstborn of Egypt; His love endures forever. And brought Israel out from among them; His love endures forever. With a mighty hand and out-stretched arm; His love endures forever.

Picture God's mighty hand and outstretched arm. Ask for His deliverance either for yourself, for a friend, or for our Nation.

SALVATION

Verses 23–24: To the One who remembered us in our low estate; His love endures forever. And freed us from our enemies; His love endures forever.

Thank Him for remembering and freeing you.

❦ Psalm 139

Omniscient

Verses 1–4: O Lord, you have searched me and you know me. You know when I sit and when I rise; you perceive my thoughts from afar. You discern my going out and my lying down; you are familiar with all my ways. Before a word is on my tongue you know it completely, O Lord.

We may sometimes think it intrusive that God knows us so completely, but it is not in a meddlesome way. He knows us because He can do no other. Like the sculptor knows his statue and like the composer knows his music, God knows us completely (and loves us anyway). Think About His Love.

Omnipresent

Verses 5–10: You hem me in—behind and before; you have laid your hand upon me. Such knowledge is too wonderful for me, too lofty for me to attain. Where can I go from your Spirit? Where can I flee from your presence? If I go up to the heavens, you are there; if I make my bed in the depths, you are there. If I rise on the wings of the dawn, if I settle on the far side of the sea, even there your hand will guide me, your right hand will hold me fast.

Omnipotent

Verses 13–14: You created my inmost being; you knit me together in my mother's womb. I praise you because I am fearfully and wonderfully made; your works are wonderful, I know that full well.

Ask God to create something great with your life. Pray this closing prayer:

Verses 23–24: Search me, O God, and know my heart; test me and know my anxious thoughts. See if there is any offensive way in me, and lead me in the way everlasting.

Try to memorize this prayer, and pray it often today.

Psalm 145 ❧

KING
Verse 1: I will exalt you, my God the King; I will praise your name for ever and ever.

Imagine being a citizen in a country who had a king. What would you as his subject do in his presence? What honor would you show? What attitude would you display? Exalt the Lord in this way.

GREAT AND MIGHTY
Verses 3–4: Great is the Lord and most worthy of praise; his greatness no one can fathom. One generation will commend your works to another; they will tell of your mighty acts.

We are to "commend His works and speak of His mighty acts." Think of two of God's mighty acts. Speak them out loud. Determine to tell them to someone today.

FAITHFUL
Verses 13–15: Your kingdom is an everlasting kingdom, and your dominion endures through all generations. The Lord is faithful to all his promises and loving toward all he has made. The Lord upholds all those who fall and lifts up all who are bowed down. The eyes of all look to you, and you give them their food at the proper time.

Pick your favorite promise of God, and remember again that He is still faithful to it.

HIS NAME IS HOLY
Verse 21: My mouth will speak in praise of the Lord. Let every creature praise his holy name for ever and ever.

Let your mouth speak in praise of the Lord. Praise his name because it is holy. Speak the names of God with reverence.

NEW TESTAMENT

Matthew 6:31–34 ❦

Do Not Worry

Verses 31–32: "So do not worry, saying, 'What shall we eat?' or 'What shall we drink?' or 'What shall we wear?' For the pagans run after all these things, and your heavenly Father knows that you need them."

"Lord, I confess that I have acted more like a pagan than a child of Yours, because I have been running after things. I have been consumed with survival rather than with pleasing you. I confess that I have worried instead of trusted. I acknowledge that worry is a sin, because You command against it. I now cast my future survival upon You. I am your responsibility. I trust You to provide for me. I will do my part, but ultimately I am trusting in You, not me."

Seek His Kingdom

Verse 33: "But seek first his kingdom and his righteousness, and all these things will be given to you as well."

Ask these questions in each arena of your life:
1. "How can I put Your kingdom first in my…"
2. "How can I be more righteous in my…"

Family	Hobbies
Work	Ministry
Private life	Finances

Live In Today

Verse 34: "Therefore do not worry about tomorrow, for tomorrow will worry about itself. Each day has enough trouble of its own."

Decide to live in and enjoy this moment with God. Surrender to Him; appreciate Him; depend upon Him; boast of Him; flatter Him.

❦ Matthew 8:23–27

Rest In God

Verses 23–24: Then he got into the boat and his disciples followed him. Without warning, a furious storm came up on the lake, so that the waves swept over the boat. But Jesus was sleeping.

Following Christ does not guarantee "smooth sailing." Only when your life is completely in the hands of another can you "sleep through the storm." Take time to give Christ ownership. Put Him on the throne of your life. Picture yourself bowing at his feet, offering all you have to Him.

Trust In God

Verses 25–26: The disciples went and woke him, saying, "Lord, save us! We're going to drown!" He replied, "You of little faith, why are you so afraid?" Then he got up and rebuked the winds and the waves, and it was completely calm.

Christ says that to be afraid shows my faith is small. Is worry the proof that I am still trusting in my own strength and abilities? List your worries on a piece of paper…. Decide now to choose faith rather than fear for each specific one.

Worship God

Verse 27: The disciples were amazed and asked, "What kind of man is this? Even the winds and the waves obey him!"

Speak your amazement of God to God. Thumb through Psalms and speak any statements of praise that you find.

Matthew 9:18 ❧

Seek Christ
While he was saying this, a ruler came

Jairus, a synagogue ruler, went against the flow of popular opinion and went to find Jesus. What did it take to get him to this point? His daughter had died. Do I have the strength to seek Christ even when it is unpopular? Must God engineer a motivation stronger than my fear, or can I choose now to own Christ. Think of the times when you are less likely to speak up for Christ, and pray for courage and strength.

Humble Yourself
…and knelt before him

Move out of the chair you are sitting in and invite Christ to sit there. Get on your knees now and speak words of reverence to Him; words of confession; compare and contrast.

Speak Your Faith
…and said "My daughter has just died. But come and put your hand on her, and she will live."

Speak your faith in the different concerns of your life (provision; deliverance; salvation of others; future; strength; etc.):

"Lord, I believe you can _____."

End your time today by reading or reciting one of the creeds of the Faith.

❧ Matthew 11:28–30

Come To Christ
Verse 28a: "Come to me, all you who are weary and burdened,"

Picture yourself walking up to Christ. Leave behind the things that tire you. Walk away from the things that weigh you down. Turn your palms over, and symbolically let the cares and worries slip out of your hands. Step out of your routine for a few minutes to spend time with Christ.

Come Let Us Worship

Receive Rest
Verse 28b: "and I will give you rest."

Turn your palms up and cup them together. Ask God to replace your anxieties with his rest. Ask him to fill you up again with his Holy Spirit. Ask for his eternal perspective on things. Take time to receive his rest.

Take His Yoke And Learn
Verses 29–30: "Take my yoke upon you and learn from me, for I am gentle and humble in heart, and you will find rest for your souls. For my yoke is easy and my burden is light."

Think on his gentleness. Ask the Holy Spirit where you could employ his gentleness with others…

Think on his humble heart. Ask the Holy Spirit to point out where you acted pridefully…

Think on the load you are carrying. If it feels bulky and heavy, perhaps you are carrying the wrong load. Ask the Holy Spirit to guide you to whatever corrections are necessary.

Matthew 28:16–19 ❦

The Great Commission

They Obeyed

Verse 16: Then the eleven disciples went to Galilee, to the mountain where Jesus had told them to go.

In other words, they went *where* they were supposed to, *when* they were supposed to. As you come to God today, take time for examination so that you, too, will come in obedience. Commit yourself once again to living by God's rules.

They Worshiped

Verse 17: When they saw him, they worshiped Him.

Pray that the Lord would open your eyes, to see Him. Pray that the Holy Spirit would provide words of adoration, to speak to Him. Speak them now.

His Authority

Verse 18: All authority in heaven and on earth has been given to me.

All authority! This means that nothing is outside His control; nothing happens without His knowledge; nothing is too difficult for Him. Speak your requests to Him.

His Compassion

Verse 19: Therefore go and make disciples of all nations.

Stop now and pray for those in your circle of influence who need to know Christ. Pray also for people who have never heard of Jesus. Pray for Muslim peoples; pray for those in cults; pray for Hindu peoples; pray for Communists; pray for Buddhist peoples; ask God to use you in his great commission today.

❦ Luke 7:3–10

Verses 3–5: The centurion heard of Jesus and sent some elders of
the Jews to him, asking him to come and heal his servant. When
they came to Jesus, they pleaded earnestly with him, "This man
deserves to have you do this, because he loves our nation and has
built our synagogue."

Employ Humility

Verses 6–7a: So Jesus went with them. He was not far from the
house when the centurion sent friends to say to him: "Lord,
don't trouble yourself, for I do not deserve to have you come
under my roof. That is why I did not even consider myself
worthy to come to you."

Lay yourself low before Christ. "You are great, I am small; You
are strong, I am weak;" etc.

Exercise Faith

Verse 7b: "But say the word and my servant will be healed."

Take the time and courage to pray for some impossible things.

Acknowledge Authority

Verses 8–10: "For I myself am a man under authority, with sol-
diers under me. I tell this one, 'Go,' and he goes; and that one,
'Come,' and he comes. I say to my servant, 'Do this,' and he
does it." When Jesus heard this, he was amazed at him, and
turning to the crowd following him, he said, "I tell you, I have
not found such great faith even in Israel." Then the men who
had been sent returned to the house and found the servant well.

List Christ's titles/descriptions of royalty, i.e., King; Majestic;
Lord; etc. Speak these in reverence to Him. Acknowledge His
sovereignty over your life.

Luke 7:36–38 ❧

Seek Christ

Verses 36–37: Now one of the Pharisees invited Jesus to have dinner with him, so he went to the Pharisee's house and reclined at the table. When a woman who had lived a sinful life in that town learned that Jesus was eating at the Pharisee's house, she brought an alabaster jar of perfume,

Examine your motives for meeting with God today. Are you really seeking Christ? Are you easing your conscience? Are you accomplishing a goal? Set your heart and mind to call out for Christ. Take hold of Him in prayer. Seek Him earnestly.

Sorrow For Sin

Verse 38a: and as she stood behind him at his feet weeping, she began to wet his feet with her tears.

Does the presence of Christ arouse in you a godly sorrow for sin? If not, pray for conviction. If so, pray a prayer of confession.

Selflessness

Verse 38b: Then she wiped them with her hair and kissed them,

She didn't care about her hair; she didn't care what people were saying; she didn't care how she would look when she walked home. Get alone and worship Christ as whole-heartedly and selflessly as you can.

Honor

Verse 38c: and poured perfume on them.

Find a costly way to honor Christ. Devise a plan; i.e., pray through lunch; pray through your whole commute; give a secret cash donation; etc.

❧ Luke 9:20–25

HIS IDENTITY

Verse 20: "But what about you?" he asked. "Who do you say that I am?" Peter answered, "The Christ of God."

Say out loud, "Jesus, You are the Christ of God," three times. Then begin to speak some of His titles and descriptions from Scripture as your prayer of praise today.

HIS MISSION

Verse 22: "The Son of Man must suffer many things and be rejected by the elders, chief priests and teachers of the law, and he must be killed and on the third day be raised to life."

Stop now and take complete control of your mind. Meditate on his torture. Meditate on his rejection. Meditate on his crucifixion. Meditate on his resurrection.

HIS REQUIREMENT

Verses 23–25: "If anyone would come after me, he must deny himself and take up his cross daily and follow me. For whoever wants to save his life will lose it, but whoever loses his life for me will save it. What good is it for a man to gain the whole world, and yet lose or forfeit his very self?"

Am I following after Christ? Do I really want to follow Christ? The *right* answer is yes, but what is the *true* answer? What is *my* answer? In which areas am I denying myself? How, practically, am I dying for others?

Grab paper and pencil, and draw a line down the middle of the page. On one side write the ways you are "saving" your life and on the other write the ways you are "losing" your life for Christ. According to the page are you forfeiting your kingdom or forfeiting your soul?

John 1:1–4 ❧

Christ Is God
Verse 1: The Word was with God, and the Word *was* God.

"Jesus, I worship You as God. I bow down only to You. You are the Lord of the ages. You are the great I Am. You are Master. You are Savior. You are God. Amen!"

Christ Is Eternal
Verse 2: He was with God in the beginning.

Christ is God, and Christ is eternal. Indeed, Christ would not be God if He were not eternal. If anyone or anything preceded Him, He would be less than God. As it is, this Christ Whom we worship had no beginning and will have no end.

"Lord, I am grateful that You are so much greater than I. I know You can do anything. Here are the people I need You to intervene with so that they will be in your eternity."

(List people for whom you are praying.)

He Is Creator
Verse 3: Through him all things were made; without him nothing was made that has been made.

Think through and thank Him for the many different aspects of His creation. Worship Christ the Creator.

Christ Is Life And Light
Verse 4: In Him was life, and that life was the light of men.

In other words, Christ is the very essence of our existence. The first thing He created was light, and this is somehow life to us. This Jesus, this Word, this Light, is our God!

Sing: "Thy Word" (Also sing "Je-sus is a lamp unto my feet")

❦ John 3:16

For God so loved the world that he gave his one and only Son, that whoever believes in him shall not perish but have eternal life.

THE REASON FOR THE GIFT
We know that Christ is God's gift to us because "God *gave* His only begotten Son."

Jesus was given because "God so loved the world." The reason for the gift of Christ is the love of God. Think about His love.

THE REQUIREMENT OF THE GIFT
This gift of God is free, but it is not cheap. It requires faith. The verse says that "Whoever *believes* in Him." This gift requires that I believe in Christ.

Recite or read a creed.

THE RECIPIENT OF THE GIFT
The reason for the gift is love; the requirement, belief. But to whom is the gift given? The Bible says "*Whoever* believes." The recipient of the gift is anyone who will accept it. Anyone! This gift is given to sinners. Christianity is one big come-as-you-are party.

Pray in faith for the salvation of those in your circle of influence who need Christ.

THE REWARD OF THE GIFT
Finally, John 3:16 tells us that this is the gift that "keeps on giving." It says that the reward of the gift is that "whosoever believes will not perish, but will have everlasting life." Along with our salvation we receive a guarantee of eternal life.

Bow and praise Him for your eternal reward; for its hope; for no more pain; for the end of death; for freedom from sin.

Acts 2:29–33 ❦

Christ's Perfection

Verses 29–32: "Brothers, I can tell you confidently that the patriarch David died and was buried, and his tomb is here to this day. But he was a prophet and knew that God had promised him on oath that he would place one of his descendants on his throne. Seeing what was ahead, he spoke of the resurrection of the Christ, that he was not abandoned to the grave, nor did his body see decay. God has raised this Jesus to life, and we are all witnesses of the fact."

If the Christ had stayed dead, He would have taken his place in history next to the great moral teachers. But, his resurrection proves his deity and sets Him apart in the universe. Speak words of gratitude as you celebrate the resurrection of Christ, the source and proof of our hope.

Christ's Position

Verse 33a: "Exalted to the right hand of God."

Speak words of exaltation to Him. "Lord, You are higher than _____; greater than _____; more powerful than _____; holier than _____;" etc.

Christ's Provision

Verse 33b: "He has received from the Father the promised Holy Spirit and has poured out what you now see and hear."

This same Holy Spirit has been poured out upon us. If we have the Holy Spirit, we have the power to overcome; we have the courage to endure; we have the gifts to serve our church; we have the ability to love the unlovely; we have the words to say to the skeptic; we have the comfort that we and others are starving for. Pray for the Lord to fill you with his Holy Spirit for the sake of others.

❦ Romans 8:1–6

PARDONED

Verses 1–2: Therefore, there is now no condemnation for those who are in Christ Jesus, because through Christ Jesus the law of the Spirit of life set me free from the law of sin and death.

Take time to remember the first time you experienced the complete forgiveness of God, or imagine what being pardoned from Death Row would be like. Give thanks.

JUSTIFIED

Verses 3–4: For what the law was powerless to do in that it was weakened by the sinful nature, God did by sending his own Son in the likeness of sinful man to be a sin offering. And so he condemned sin in sinful man, in order that the righteous requirements of the law might be fully met in us, who do not live according to the sinful nature but according to the Spirit.

Justified means "just-*if*-I'd" never sinned. "Thank you, Lord for meeting the standard for me, knowing I could not. Let me live according to the Spirit today."

SANCTIFIED

Verses 5–6: Those who live according to the sinful nature have their minds set on what that nature desires; but those who live in accordance with the Spirit have their minds set on what the Spirit desires. The mind of sinful man is death, but the mind controlled by the Spirit is life and peace;

Sanctified means "set-apart for a holy use." "Sanctify me today, Lord, to do your will here on earth. Live through me."

Romans 12:1–2 ✿

View His Mercy
Verse 1a: Therefore, I urge you, brothers, in view of God's mercy,

Take time to confess deeply. Recite each shortcoming in view of His mercy:

> "You have overlooked my…"

(ingratitude; bitterness; anger; jealousy; greed; lust; hurry; motivations; selfishness; lies; etc.)

Offer Yourself
Verse 1b: …to offer your bodies as living sacrifices, holy and pleasing to God—this is your spiritual act of worship.

> Picture an altar which is set in the presence of God.
> > Climb up onto it!
> Picture the Cross with Christ still on it.
> > Grab the bottom of it!
> Picture your possessions in one big pile.
> > Light it!

Be Transformed
Verse 2a: Do not conform any longer to the pattern of this world, but be transformed by the renewing of your mind.

Dear Lord,
Society asks "how much are you earning?" Your Word asks "how much are you giving?" Society says "promote yourself!" Your Word says "deny yourself!" Society asks "how many know your face?" Your Word asks "how many know your touch?" Society says "go get what you want!" Your Word says "help others get what they need!" Society asks "will you compromise?" Your Word asks "will you sacrifice." Transform my mind, Lord.

❧ II Corinthians 1:2–6

Remember His Grace

Verse 2: Grace and peace to you from God our Father and the Lord Jesus Christ.

Meditate on God's grace.…Meditate on God's peace.…
Acknowledge God as Father.…Acknowledge Jesus as Lord.…

Remember His Compassion

Verse 3: Praise be to the God and Father of our Lord Jesus Christ, the Father of compassion and the God of all comfort,

Recall the compassion and comfort you have received from God. Speak specific words of thanksgiving to Him for these gifts.

Remember His Comfort

Verses 4–5: who comforts us in all our troubles, so that we can comfort those in any trouble with the comfort we ourselves have received from God. For just as the sufferings of Christ flow over into our lives, so also through Christ our comfort overflows.

What is the most difficult thing you have ever been through? Ask God to lead you to someone else who is struggling with the same thing, so that God can use your pain for His Kingdom.

Remember Others

Verse 6: If we are distressed, it is for your comfort and salvation; if we are comforted, it is for your comfort, which produces in you patient endurance of the same sufferings we suffer.

Pray for those in your circle of influence who need Christ. Wrestle for their souls; beg God to move in these lives; determine to try again to share God's good news with them.

II Corinthians 1:14–22

Have Eternal Perspective
Verse 14: As you have understood us in part, you will come to understand fully that you can boast of us just as we will boast of you in the day of the Lord Jesus.

Inventory your life from an eternal perspective. What eternal things are you doing? What necessary but non-eternal things? What eternally wasteful things?

Affirm God's Will
Verse 17b: Do I make my plans in a worldly manner so that in the same breath I say, "Yes, yes" and "No, no?"

Ask God how *He* would have you serve Him in the future.

Glorify Christ
Verses 19–20: For the Son of God, Jesus Christ, who was preached among you by me and Silas and Timothy, was not "Yes" and "No," but in him it has always been "Yes." For no matter how many promises God has made, they are "Yes" in Christ. And so through him the "Amen" is spoken by us to the glory of God.

Christ is that absolute and complete satisfaction of all the promises of God, but is He the absolute and complete satisfaction of your longings, fears, and ambitions? Ask that He would be.

Sense His Spirit
Verse 22: He anointed us, set his seal of ownership on us, and put his Spirit in our hearts as a deposit, guaranteeing what is to come.

"Lord, You have anointed me; set a seal of ownership on me; put your Holy Spirit in me as a reminder of my guaranteed eternal life! I worship You. You are majestic in holiness; an all-consuming fire; everlasting. Hallelujah!"

❦ II Corinthians 3:2–6

A Living Letter

Verses 2–3: You yourselves are our letter, written on our hearts, known and read by everybody. You show that you are a letter from Christ, the result of our ministry, written not with ink but with the Spirit of the Living God, not on tablets of stone but on tablets of human hearts.

What message has the Spirit of God written on your heart? What has He done in you that you could not do in yourself? What is the most outstanding thing Christ has done for you? Say it as a praise! "Christ has: forgiven; healed; saved; guided; comforted; filled;" etc.

Confident

Verses 4–5: Such confidence as this is ours through Christ before God. Not that we are competent in ourselves to claim anything for ourselves, but our confidence comes from God.

Think back over the last 3 days. Has your confidence been only in Christ, or has it been in lesser things? Spend time in confession and re-commitment if necessary.

Competent

Verse 6: He has made us competent as ministers of a new covenant—not of the letter but of the Spirit; for the letter kills, but the Spirit gives life.

Father, You can make me able to tell others of Your loving promises. I want to influence, rather than impress, those around me. Let the letter of my life be an accurate one. Let me be a life-giver. Don't let my abilities, assets, or personality get in the way of Your Spirit. Amen!

II Corinthians 6:18–7:1 ✤

The Promises
Verse 18: "I will receive you. I will be a Father to you, and you will be my sons and daughters."

Imagine yourself as a homeless person looking for shelter. The promise is that we will be received by God. Not only received, but also adopted. He gathers us to Himself as a bird gathers her chicks under wing. This is what God has done with us. Do you need more reason than that to praise Him? Speak words of appreciation and gratitude to Him.

The Admonition
Verse 1a: Since we have these promises, dear friends, (that being the promises of being received and adopted) let us purify ourselves from everything that contaminates body and spirit,

Take time now to "purify yourself from everything that contaminates body and spirit."
Silently confess your sins to the Lord….
Confess your silent rage, or your hidden bitterness.…
Deal ruthlessly with your bad habits.…
Turn from the sins which society has made acceptable.
Sins like greed…a work-a-holic lifestyle…hoarding…gluttony…self-reliance.
Purify yourself from *every thing* that contaminates.

The Motive
Verse 1b: perfecting holiness out of reverence for God.

God deserves our praise because He has received us and adopted us, but He deserves our holiness because it is a sign of our reverence for God. Revere Him! Lift Him up! Commit to a lifestyle of holiness.

❦ Galatians 5:22–25

Confess
Verses 22–23: The fruit of the Spirit is love, joy, peace, patience, kindness, goodness, faithfulness, gentleness and self-control. Against such things there is no law.

Take a moment to evaluate yourselves in light of this list. Slip your name in before each characteristic. Silently confess your shortcomings.

Surrender
Verse 24: Those who belong to Christ Jesus have crucified the sinful nature with its passions and desires.

Those who belong to Christ! Do you belong to Christ? Does He have complete ownership of you at this very moment? Go through each compartment of your life. Pray, and give Him complete control of each area.

Worship
Verse 25: Since we live by the Spirit let us keep in step with the Spirit.

"Lord, let me 'keep step with the Spirit' by honoring You and by bearing witness today of Who you are. Spirit, enable me to praise, that I might honor God."

Speak out loud "Lord, You are _____."

Insert some of the attributes of God.

Ephesians 1:3–8

He Blessed Us

Verse 3: Praise be to the God and Father of our Lord Jesus Christ, who has blessed us in the heavenly realms with every spiritual blessing in Christ.

Enumerate his spiritual blessings. Speak praises to God with words of gratitude for his blessings.

He Chose, Adopted, And Predestined Us

Verses 4–5: For he chose us in him before the creation of the world to be holy and blameless in his sight. In love he predestined us to be adopted as his sons through Jesus Christ, in accordance with his pleasure and will—

Imagine being the worst athlete in the school, and getting picked first to be on the best athlete's team. Imagine great parents choosing you from an entire orphanage. Imagine someone rigging the game of life so that you couldn't lose (unless you insisted on it). Read these verses again, slowly, out loud, inserting "me" for "us."

He Gave Us Grace And Redemption

Verses 6–8: to the praise of his glorious grace which he has freely given us in the One he loves. In him we have redemption through his blood, the forgiveness of sins, in accordance with the riches of God's grace that he lavished on us with all wisdom and understanding.

God didn't give us just enough grace to make the grade. He lavished it upon us! Thank Him for forgiveness; newness; victory; guidance; heaven; rest; provision; assurance; strength; protection.

❧ Ephesians 3:16–19

His Power

Verse 16: I pray that out of his glorious riches he may strengthen you with power through his Spirit in your inner being,

Do you feel powerful today? Is there an area of your life where you have been relying upon your own power rather than God's? Don't ask "How much of the Holy Spirit do I have?", but rather, "How much of me does the *Holy Spirit* have?"

His Presence

Verse 17: so that Christ may dwell in your hearts through faith.

Recognize and acknowledge Christ's presence in you at this very moment.

Speak out loud some words of faith; i.e., "I believe Christ is the only Son of God; I believe the Holy Bible is His only word; I believe Jesus is the only way to heaven."

His Process

Verses 18–19: And I pray that you, being rooted and established in love may have power, together with all the saints, to grasp how wide and long and high and deep is the love of Christ, and to know this love that surpasses knowledge—that you may be filled to the measure of all the fullness of God.

Has your appreciation of His love grown? Are you grasping more of His graciousness? Is your love and worship of God greater than it was a week ago? A year ago? Rate your understanding of His love for you on a scale from one to ten. Write it down, then compare your mark in a week.

Philippians 2:1–11 ❦

UNITY

Verses 1–2: If you have any encouragement from being united with Christ, if any comfort from his love, if any fellowship with the Spirit, if any tenderness and compassion, then make my joy complete by being like-minded, having the same love, being one in spirit and purpose.

Like minded; one Spirit and purpose! "Lord, reveal any rebellious attitudes in me, and remove them."

HUMILITY

Verses 3–4: Do nothing out of selfishness or empty conceit, but with humility of mind let each of you consider one another more important than yourselves. Do not look out merely for your own interests, but also for the interests of others.

Humble yourself through "compare and contrast:" "You are great, I am small. You are holy, I am _____." etc.

REMEMBER

Verses 5–8: Have this mind among yourselves which is yours in Christ Jesus, Who, Though He was in the form of God, did not count equality with God a thing to be grasped, but emptied Himself, taking the form of a servant. And being found in human form, He humbled Himself and became obedient unto death, even death on a cross.

Meditate on what Christ did on your behalf. Are you willing to do that for the sake of others? Pray that it would be so.

HONOR

Verses 9–11: Therefore God has highly exalted Him, and bestowed upon Him a name that is above every name, that at the name of Jesus every knee should bow, in heaven and on earth and under the earth, and every tongue confess that Jesus Christ is Lord, to the glory of God the Father.

Kneel and sing: "He Is Lord"

❧ I Timothy 1:15–17

Humility

Verse 15: Here is a trustworthy saying that deserves full acceptance: Christ Jesus came into the world to save sinners—of whom I am the worst.

Repeat twice the words of Paul: "Christ Jesus came into the world to save sinners, of whom I am the worst." Pray:

Dear God,
Your wish is my command. Your will is my purpose. Your work is my joy. Your Word is my authority. Your Kingdom is my home. Your plans are my aspirations. Your standards are my goals. Your worth is my motivation. Your sovereignty is my assurance. Your power is my rest. Your character is my boast.

Amnesty

Verse 16: But for that very reason I was shown mercy so that in me, the worst of sinners, Christ Jesus might display his unlimited patience as an example for those who would believe on him and receive eternal life.

Think: "I am an example of Christ's mercy. When people see me they should think that perhaps there is also hope for them. Am I giving Christ the credit, or do I secretly think that I'm not that bad. Thank you, Lord, for your mercy."

Majesty

Verse 17: Now to the King eternal, immortal, invisible, the only God, be honor and glory for ever and ever. Amen.

"I, too, Lord, want to add my words of adoration to these verses. You are purer than _____; more loving than _____; greater than _____; more faithful than _____. Amen."

Hebrews 1:1–9 ❦

Exactly God

Verses 1–3: In the past God spoke to our forefathers through the prophets at many times and in various ways, but in these last days he has spoken to us by his Son, whom he appointed heir of all things, and through whom he made the universe. The Son is the radiance of God's glory and the exact representation of his being, sustaining all things by his powerful word.

"Jesus, You inherit all things; the universe was made through You; You are God; Your word is powerful and sustaining. Let your word dwell in me today."

Worthy Of Worship

Verse 6: When God brings his first-born into the world, he says, "Let all God's angels worship him."

Even when Christ became Man, He was worthy of the angels' worship. Speak things that are only true about Jesus. "You are eternal; You are Creator;" etc.

Eternal

Verse 8: But about the Son he says, "Your throne, O God, will last for ever and ever, and righteousness will be the scepter of your kingdom.

Imagine Christ the Eternal King there with you, and let your heart lead you to respond.

Righteous

Verse 9: You have loved righteousness and hated wickedness; therefore God, your God has set you above your companions by anointing you with the oil of joy."

God-the-Father calls Jesus "God!" So should we. "Jesus, You are God; not a god, but the Only True Living God!"

❦ Hebrews 12:1–3

Untangle Yourself

Verse 1: Since we are surrounded by such a great cloud of witnesses, let us throw off everything that hinders and the sin that so easily entangles, and let us run with perseverance the race marked out for us.

Take the time to lay aside the things that entangle you.
"Cast your cares upon Him" (I Peter 5:7).

Give Him your worries.
Confess your secret sins.
Let go of your materialism.
Sacrifice your need to be accepted by the world.

Fix Your Eyes Upon Christ

Verse 2: Let us fix our eyes on Jesus, the author and perfecter of our faith, who for the joy set before him endured the cross, scorning its shame, and sat down at the right hand of the throne of God.

This verse says some amazing things about Jesus, but what it says to us is quite simple: "fix your eyes on Jesus." Close your eyes, and:

Think about Jesus   Remember Jesus
Meditate upon Jesus   Consider Jesus
Focus upon Jesus

Consider Him

Verse 3: Consider him who endured such opposition from sinful men, so that you will not grow weary and lose heart.

Think on the example of Christ.

Restate your resolve to following Christ.
Declare again your intention to stay faithful.
Commit anew to a lifestyle of dependence on Him.

1 Peter 1:2–6

I Am Chosen, Sanctified, And Obedient

Verse 2: …who have been chosen according to the foreknowledge of God the Father, through the sanctifying work of the Spirit, for obedience to Jesus Christ and sprinkling by his blood: Grace and peace be yours in abundance.

Thank the Father for *choosing* you. Acknowledge the Holy Spirit for His *sanctifying* (drawing you from sin toward holiness) work in you. Honor Christ for making *obedience* possible through His redemption.

Praise Him

Verses 3–5: Praise be to the God and Father of our Lord Jesus Christ! In his great mercy he has given us new birth into a living hope through the resurrection of Jesus Christ from the dead, and into an inheritance that can never perish, spoil or fade—kept in heaven for you, who through faith are shielded by God's power until the coming of the salvation that is ready to be revealed in the last time.

New birth is a *work* that God has done in us; an inheritance is a *hope* that God gives to us; shielded by God's power is God's *guarantee* on the matter. Offer the Lord words of gratitude for His work in you.

Rejoice

Verse 6: In this you greatly rejoice, though now for a little while you may have had to suffer grief in all kinds of trials.

Rejoicing is not a feeling that you must conjure up, but rather, it is a decision you must make; an attitude you must adopt. Decide now to rejoice! Say these things out loud:

> In spite of suffering, I choose to rejoice.
> In spite of grief, I choose to rejoice.
> In spite of all kinds of trials, I choose to rejoice.

❦ I Peter 1:8–9

Love Him
Verse 8a: Though you have not seen him, you love him;

Express your love to Christ by taking the time right now to get paper and pencil and write Him a letter. Write down why:
> you love Him (attributes)
> you thank Him (blessings)
> you fear him (works)

Believe And Rejoice In Him
Verse 8b: and even though you do not see him now, you believe in him and are filled with an inexpressible and glorious joy,

Also on that paper write what you believe as an act of faith. Write your beliefs about: (stay simple)

| the person of Christ | the Holy Bible |
| future inheritance | salvation |

Take time to rejoice. Do something tangible (shout; sing; recite; pray; dance; cheer; lift hands; clap; read aloud; give).

Receive Him
Verse 9: for your are receiving the goal of your faith, the salvation of your souls.

On that same piece of paper list the fruit that show you are saved. Are you: (Galatians 5:22–23)

more loving?	more godly?
more joyful?	more faithful?
more peaceful?	more gentle?
more patient?	more self-controlled?
more kind?	

What would others write about you?

I Peter 1:13–16

Prepare Mind

Verse 13: Therefore, prepare your minds for action; be self-controlled; set your hope fully on the grace to be given you when Jesus Christ is revealed.

Take a deep breath and decided you will not rush through your time with God. Ask for the mind set of a servant....

Ask The Holy Spirit to illumine an area in your life which is not under His control. Yield now!

Remind yourself that you have not, will not, and cannot do anything to earn your way to heaven. Set your hope totally on His grace.

Do Not Conform

Verse 14: As obedient children, do not conform to the evil desires you had when you lived in ignorance.

Make a mental list of the evidence which proves you are a follower of Christ. Is it convincing? If not, what needs to change?

Be Holy

Verses 15–16: But just as he who called you is holy, so be holy in all you do; for it is written: "Be holy, because I am holy."

Speak words of reverence and adoration to God. End with:

"Holy, Holy, Holy Lord; God of power and might.
 Heaven and earth are filled with your glory.
  Hosanna in the highest!
Blessed is He who comes in the name of the Lord.
 Hosanna in the highest!"

❦ I Peter 2:4–6

Choose Christ

Verse 4: You come to Him, the living Stone—rejected by men but chosen by God and precious to him.

Speak these words out loud: "I reject Buddha, who is dead. I reject Confucius, who is dead. I reject Mohammed, who is dead. I reject Joseph Smith, founder of Mormonism, who is dead. I reject Mary Baker Eddy, founder of Christian Science, who is dead. I reject Russell, founder of Jehovah's Witnesses, who is dead.

I choose and believe in Jesus Christ the Lord, Who is alive!

Offer Spiritual Sacrifices

Verse 5: You also, like living stones, are being built into a spiritual house to be a holy priesthood, offering spiritual sacrifices acceptable to God through Jesus Christ.

Offer these spiritual sacrifices to God:
- The sacrifice of Sin (list sins)
- The sacrifice of Praise (speak His attributes)
- The sacrifice of Self (list goals and dreams)
- The sacrifice of Resources (decide to give an unnoticed gift to your church)

Trust In Him

Verse 6: See, I lay a stone in Zion, a chosen and precious cornerstone, and the one who trusts in him will never be put to shame.

Think of areas in your life in which you are strong, prepared, confident, etc. These are areas in which you may be trusting in yourself rather than God. Go back through the list, and go to God for each area.

II Peter 1:4 ❦

Receive His Promises
Through these he has given us his very great and precious promises,

Recite slowly as many promises of God as come to mind. Let each one's meaning sink deeply into your heart. Ask God to let each promise refresh your spirit.

Participate In His Nature
...so that through them you may participate in the divine nature

The Holy Spirit lives within each believer. I Corinthians 3:16 says that each is a temple of God. Set your heart and mind to be very aware of The Holy Spirit's presence now. Acknowledge Him. Surrender to Him. Ask Him to guide and teach you. Ask Him to comfort or counsel or pray to the Father on your behalf.

Escape Corruption
...and escape the corruption in the world caused by evil desires.

Ask The Holy Spirit to grow in you a hatred of all sin. Ask Him to help you view your sin as something which keeps you from God's blessings and plan; something which robs your joy and slows your growth. Ask The Holy Spirit to convict you now of anything which offends Him.

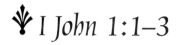 *I John 1:1–3*

Christ Is The Word Of Life

Verse 1: That which was from the beginning, which we have heard, which we have seen with our eyes, which we have looked at and our hands have touched—this we proclaim concerning the Word of life.

"Christ, You are the very essence of life. You are at the core of creation and give meaning and purpose to every thing. Without You, my life is gibberish: meaningless mumblings; moronic meanderings. You brought order to the chaos of my soul; purpose to my mind; peace to my heart. I praise You with all that I am. Amen!"

Christ Is Eternal Life

Verse 2: The life appeared; we have seen it and testify to it, and we proclaim to you the eternal life, which was with the Father and has appeared to us.

"Christ, You are eternal life. To live forever is to live in the light of Your Presence. You are Good Shepherd; Lover Of My Soul; Joy; Soul-Mate; Hero; Healing Oil. I want to live with You."

Fellowship With Christ

Verse 3: We proclaim to you what we have seen and heard, so that you also may have fellowship with us. And our fellowship is with the Father and with his Son, Jesus Christ.

Ask God to help you continue in fellowship with Him all day. Choose something you look at often, and move it out of place to remind you to tune your heart to praise the Living Christ.

Ideas: turn a watch or desk calendar upside down; move a desk accessory; turn a picture on its side; set your watch to beep every hour.

OLD TESTAMENT

❧ I Chronicles 16:23–29

SING

Verse 23: Sing to the Lord, all the Earth; proclaim his salvation day after day.

In an "alone" place, sing a song of praise to the Lord.

DECLARE

Verse 24: Declare his glory among the nations, his marvelous deeds among all peoples.

Speak aloud the marvelous deeds He has done in you. "He has loved me; He has forgiven me; He has healed me."

GOD IS WORTHY

Verses 25–27: For great is the Lord and most worthy of praise; he is to be feared above all gods. For all the gods of the nations are idols, but the Lord made the heavens. Splendor and majesty are before him; strength and joy in his dwelling place.

"Lord, definitions cannot encompass You; mental pictures of You are not beautiful enough; descriptions of You are not marvelous enough; traditions of You are not complete enough; experience with You does not reveal enough; study of You does not explain enough. All I can do is to be amazed, and to exalt Your name."

ASCRIBE AND BRING AN OFFERING

Verses 28–29: Ascribe to the Lord, O families of nations, ascribe to the Lord glory and strength. Ascribe to the Lord the glory due his name. Bring an offering and come before him; worship the Lord in the splendor of his holiness.

Speak out loud some of the many facets of the Jewel that is God. "You are powerful; You are kind;" etc. Give an offering.

II Chronicles 7:14 🌱

If my people, who are called by My Name

"Lord, I am called by your name: Christ-ian. Help me to live up to my name."

Will humble themselves

"Dear Lord, You are great, I am small. You are holy, I am unholy. You are strong, I am weak. You are unshakable, I am fragile. I humble myself before You."

And pray

Pray the Lord's prayer out loud.

And seek My face

"I seek You, Lord. I seek your presence. I seek your face. Come, and make Yourself at home in my schedule today. I seek you, Lord."

And turn from their wicked ways

Quietly confess your sins to the Lord.

Then will I hear from heaven,
and will forgive their sin, and heal their land

"Lord, I believe that you hear me right here, right now. I believe that You forgive me. I believe that You can do whatever You want done in my life. I praise You and stand on your promise today. Amen!"

❀ II Chronicles 20:6–15

PRAISE HIM
Verse 6: "O Lord, God of our fathers, are you not the God who is in heaven? You rule over all the kingdoms of the nations. Power and might are in your hand, and no one can withstand you."

Speak this out loud three times.

RECOUNT HIS WORKS
Verse 7: "O our God, did you not drive out the inhabitants of this land before your people Israel and give it forever to the descendants of Abraham your friend?"

Recount to Him His miracles; answered prayers; mighty works; goodness; mercies; etc.

ASK HIM
Verse 9: "…we will stand in your presence before this temple that bears your Name and will cry out to you in our distress, and you will hear us and save us."

Stand and pray: "I stand in your presence. I am a temple that bears your name. I pray to you, and believe that you will hear me and answer me. Here is what I ask of You:" (list your requests)

TRUST HIM
Verse 15: "This is what the LORD says to you: 'Do not be afraid or discouraged because of this vast army. For the battle is not yours, but God's.'"

Pray: "Instead of striving to win or receive or arrive, I decide to strive after You, O God. You are the prize I seek; the reward I need, the destination I long for."

Nehemiah 8 ❧

ASSEMBLE IN UNITY
Verse 1a: When the seventh month came and the Israelites had settled in their towns, all the people assembled as one man in the square.

How is my attitude of unity when I gather with the Body of Christ to worship the Living God? (Confess any animosity.)

REQUEST THE WORD OF GOD
Verse 1b: They told Ezra the scribe to bring out the Book of the Law of Moses, which the Lord had commanded for Israel.

I, too, want to hear and understand God as He has revealed Himself through His Word. (Pray silently to the Lord, and ask Him to speak to you through his Word.)

Sing or speak: "Thy Word"

HONOR THE WORD OF GOD
Verse 5: As he opened it, the people all stood up.

Stand to honor God's Word as you read aloud Psalm 84.

BOW DOWN AND WORSHIP
Verse 6: Ezra praised the Lord, the great God; and all the people lifted their hands and responded, "Amen! Amen!" Then they bowed down and worshiped the Lord with their faces to the ground.

Assume a position of humility, whether you bow your face, your head, your knee, or your whole body. Bow down and worship your King.

Recite as many of the Biblical names of God as you can.

❧ Proverbs 3:5–10

Trust
Verse 5: Trust in the Lord with all your heart and lean not on your own understanding;

When you got out of bed, you *trusted* that the floor would be there. When you sat down you *trusted* that the furniture would hold you. In the same way, put your *trust* in the Living God. Take the time to express to Him your complete dependence upon Him.

Acknowledge
Verse 6: In all your ways acknowledge him, and he will make your paths straight.

Speak out loud:
    I acknowledge You as my Savior.
    I acknowledge Your Lordship in my home.
    I acknowledge Your Lordship in my relationships.
    I acknowledge Your Lordship in my finances.
    I acknowledge Your Lordship in my career.

Fear The Lord
Verse 7: Do not be wise in your own eyes; fear the Lord and shun evil.

To *fear* God is to reverence Him, respect Him, and obey Him; not because He is mean or angry, but because He is God. Speak words of awe and amazement.

Honor
Verses 9–10: Honor the Lord with your wealth, with the first fruits of all your crops; then your barns will be filled with plenty, and your vats overflow with new wine.

Increase your giving by 2% for a month to honor God.

Isaiah 6:1–7

His Presence
Verse 1: In the year that King Uzziah died, I saw the Lord seated on a throne, high and exalted, and the train of his robe filled the temple.

"Lord, I want to come into your presence, but sometimes You seem far away from my world and worries. Take me by the soul and set me in your presence."

His Worship
Verses 3–4: Above him were seraphs, each with six wings: With two wings they covered their faces, with two they covered their feet, and with two they were flying. And they were calling to one another: "Holy, holy, holy is the Lord Almighty; the whole earth is full of his glory."

Fill in the blank as many times as possible with attributes of God. "God, You are _____." (strong, loving, holy)

Our Unworthiness
Verse 5: "Woe to me!" I cried, "I am ruined! For I am a man of unclean lips, and I live among a people of unclean lips, and my eyes have seen the King, the Lord Almighty."

Confess your sins to the Lord.

His Cleansing
Verses 6–7: Then one of the seraphs flew to me with a live coal in his hand, which he had taken with tongs from the altar. With it he touched my mouth and said, "See, this has touched your lips; your guilt is taken away and your sin atoned for."

Say out loud three times: "My guilt is taken away and my sin is atoned for." Repeat this promise throughout the day.

❧ Isaiah 40:22–31

SOVEREIGN

Verses 22–24: He sits enthroned above the circle of the earth, and its people are like grasshoppers. He stretches out the heavens like a canopy, and spreads them out like a tent to live in. He brings princes to naught and reduces the rulers of this world to nothing.

Is your life spinning out of control? Is it peaceful today? Do you believe God could change things in a moment if they fit His plan? Praise Him for His complete sovereignty.

CREATOR

Verses 25–26: "To whom will you compare me? Or who is my equal?" says the Holy One. Lift your eyes and look to the heavens: Who created all these? He who brings out the starry host one by one, and calls them each by name. Because of his great power and mighty strength, not one of them is missing.

God didn't create and then step away. He is still actively involved, not only in creation, but also in your life. Acknowledge his presence and work in you.

FAITHFUL

Verses 29–31: He gives strength to the weary and increases the power of the weak. Even youths grow tired and weary, and young men stumble and fall; but those who hope in the Lord will renew their strength. They will soar on wings like eagles; they will run and not grow weary, they will walk and not be faint.

"Dear Lord, I am weary and weak. Teach me to soar on your wind. I'm always flapping my wings, and I need to learn to soar. I put my hope in You only; my trust in You only; my future rests in Your hands. Renew my strength."

Isaiah 55:1–9 🌱

COME TO GOD
Verse 1: Come, all you who are thirsty, come to the waters; and you who have no money, come, buy and eat!

Stop and realize that you are coming into the presence of the Source of all life. Set your heart and mind on worshipping Him now. Imagine Him sitting with you now.

EXAMINE YOURSELF
Verse 2: Why spend money on what is not bread, and your labor on what does not satisfy? Eat what is good, and your soul will delight in the richest of fare.

Inventory the satisfaction of your soul to determine whether or not your spiritual diet is in line with God's menu.

SEEK THE LORD
Verse 6: Seek the Lord while he may be found; call on him while he is near.

Call some of His names out loud. Tell Him you are seeking Him. Tell Him you want to know Him. Speak words of adoration to Him.

MARVEL AT HIM
Verses 8–9: "For my thoughts are not your thoughts, neither are your ways my ways," declares the Lord. "As the heavens are higher than the earth, so are my ways higher than your ways and my thoughts than your thoughts."

Realizing His greatness, praise Him. Acknowledging His sovereignty, submit to Him. Imagining His wisdom, trust Him.

❦ Ezekiel 36:25–27

He Cleanses Us

Verse 25: I will sprinkle clean water on you, and you will be clean; I will cleanse you from all your impurities and from all your idols.

Do you really want to be cleansed? Are you really willing to lose your idols? Have you taken drastic steps to overcome your sin? Take the time now to be ruthless with your sin. Otherwise you are wasting your time, like washing with dirty water, or sweeping a dirt floor.

Sing: "Sanctuary"

He Gives Us A New Heart

Verse 26: I will give you a new heart and put a new spirit in you; I will remove from you your heart of stone and give you a heart of flesh.

A new heart! Why doesn't God just fix the old one? Scripture says "The heart is deceitful above all things and beyond cure. Who can understand it?" (Jeremiah 16:9) That is why God does a transplant rather than a repair. With this new heart we can now feel what He feels; respond as He would respond; forgive as He forgives; love as He would love. Is your new heart working, or do you keep it as a spare, to be used only when you want to be holy? Pray to the Lord.

Sing: "Create In Me"

He Lives Through Us

Verse 27: And I will put my Spirit in you and move you to follow my decrees and be careful to keep my laws.

Surrender control of your life once again. Picture yourself moving into the passenger seat of a car, allowing Christ to sit in the driver's seat. Now sit back, relax, and ask Him to take you wherever He wants you to be, for the rest of your life!

Malachı 3:8–11 ❦

Adapted To Church Worship

Verse 8: "Will a man rob God? Yet you rob me. But you ask 'How do we rob you?' In tithes and offerings."

"Will a man rob God? Yet you rob me. But you ask, 'How do I rob you?' In your half-hearted worship."

Verse 9: "You are under a curse—the whole nation of you—because you are robbing me."

"You are under a curse—the whole church—because you are robbing me."

Verse 10: "Bring the whole tithe into the storehouse, that there may be food in my house. Test me in this," says the Lord Almighty, "and see if I will not throw open the floodgates of heaven and pour out so much blessing that you will not have room enough for it."

"Bring your whole heart into my presence, that there may be sacrifice in my house. Test me in this," says the Lord Almighty, "and see if I will not throw open the floodgates of heaven and pour out so much blessing that you will not have room enough for it."

Verse 11: "I will prevent pests from devouring your crops, and the vines in your fields will not cast their fruit," says the Lord Almighty.

I will prevent dullness from devouring your devotions, and your spiritual fruit will not be puny and weak.

Take a spiritual inventory of the "Fruit" God has been growing, and spend time thanking Him for the growth, or repenting for the lack of it.

TOPICAL

Assurances ❧

Assurance Of Salvation
I John 5:11–13: God has given us eternal life; and this life is in his Son. He who has the Son has the life; he who does not have the Son does not have the life. These things are written in order that we may *know* that we have eternal life.

"Lord, my eternal life is not a hope, but a fact that nothing can change."

Assurance Of Answered Prayer
John 16:24: Until now you have asked for nothing in my name; ask and you will receive, that your joy may be made full.

Pray to the Lord.

Give Him your concerns.…Lift up family members who need to know Him.…Pray for whatever local, State, or Federal official that comes to mind.…Pray for the school closest to where you live.… Pray for the poor and enslaved.

Assurance Of Guidance And Victory
Proverbs 3:6: In all your ways acknowledge Him, and He will make your path straight.

"Lord, do whatever is necessary to keep me on Your path for my life."

Assurance Of Forgiveness
I John 1:9: If we confess our sins, He is faithful and just and will forgive us from sin and cleanse us from all unrighteousness.

Psalm 103:12: As far as the east is from the west, so far will I remove your sin from you.

Speak passionate praises to God, as though you were a condemned prisoner who received a pardon.

❀ The Beatitudes
Matthew 5:3–10

Blessed are the poor in spirit for theirs is the kingdom of heaven.
Disappointed are the rich in spirit; their kingdom will crumble.

Blessed are those who mourn, for they will be comforted.
Dissatisfied are those who party; God's comfort will be drowned out.

Blessed are the meek, for they will inherit the earth.
Impoverished are the arrogant; their treasure and renown will go to the meek.

Blessed are those who hunger and thirst for righteousness, for they will be filled.
Miserable are those who hunger and thirst for evil; they will remain starving and parched.

Blessed are the merciful, for they will be shown mercy.
Hopeless are the ruthless; they will receive what they have given.

Blessed are the pure in heart, for they will see God.
Blind are those with polluted hearts; they cannot recognize God.

Blessed are the peacemakers, for they will be called sons of God.
Short-sighted are the contentious; they will be avoided.

Blessed are those who are persecuted because of righteousness, for theirs is the kingdom of heaven.
Weak are those who please Man rather than God; they already have the only reward they're going to receive.

Christ The Stone ❧

Living Stone
I Peter 2:4: Come to Him, the Living Stone

Cause yourself to celebrate "Christ the Stone" as a living stone. Rejoice in the fact the He is…alive!

Stumbling Stone
Isaiah 8:14: A stone that makes men stumble, and a rock that makes them fall.

Obedience is the highest form of worship, and Christ the Stumbling Stone causes us to stop in our worship and consider our own disobedience. Which of his offensive statements do I stumble over? Which have I ignored?

"Deny yourself" (Luke 9:23)
"No one comes to the Father but by me" (John 14:6)
"Where your treasure is, there your heart also is" (Luke 12:34)
"Love your enemies" (Matthew 5:44)

Confess your sins to the Lord.

Chosen And Precious Stone
Isaiah 28:16: See, I lay a stone in Zion, a chosen and precious cornerstone, and the one who trusts in him will never be put to shame.

Speak words of love to the Chosen and Precious Christ.

Put your open palm on your lap and let it represent the foundation-stone that is Christ. Now take your other hand and symbolically gather up your entire life in your fist. Finally, symbolically set your life on Christ the Stone, and say "On Christ, the Solid Rock, I stand. All other ground is sinking sand. All other ground is sinking sand."

❦ Deity Of Christ

The common denominator of every cult, every heresy, and every false messenger is that they deny the deity of Christ. Yes, He is fully Man; and yes, He is a Friend of sinners; but the Word of God says much more about Him. First of all, we know that He is exactly God!

Exactly God
Hebrews 12:1–3: In various ways God spoke to the fathers of old, but in these last days He has spoken to us through a Son, Who reflects the glory of God and bears the very stamp of his nature.

Worship Christ as God of the universe.

Eternal
In John 8:58: "Before Abraham was, I am!"

In other words, Jesus existed in the beginning with the Father. The religious leaders knew exactly what He was saying, because they tried to kill Him for it. Acknowledge His eternal nature, and praise Him for it!

Creator
John 1:3: Through Him all things were made, and without Him nothing was made that has been made.

Worship Christ as Creator.

His Name Is Exalted
Philippians 2:9–11:…at the name of Jesus every knee should bow in heaven and on earth and under the earth, and every tongue confess that Jesus Christ is Lord, to the glory of God the Father.

Exalt His Name by listing and praising the names of the Christ!

Faith ❧

Believe In Him

Matthew 10:32: "Whoever acknowledges me before men, I will also acknowledge him before my Father in heaven."

Take the time to list as many Biblical absolutes as you can. Use this format:

"I believe _____." (in God the Father; in the resurrection; etc.)

Trust In Him

Philippians 4:6–7: Have no anxiety about anything, but in everything with prayer and thanksgiving let your requests be made known to God; and the peace of God which passes all understanding will keep your hearts and minds in Christ Jesus.

Is worry a sin? Yes! It shows that we are trusting in someone or something besides Christ.

Where is your trust and reliance right now? Is it in your job; education; IRA; personality; etc.? To get an honest answer, ask yourself what would change if Christ failed you. Once you have the answer, mentally turn your back on those things and put your faith, trust, and reliance totally in Christ. Make this transaction now.

Now, speak your requests to God, giving thanks after each request as you speak it.

Live For Him

Hebrews 11:1: Faith is being sure of what we hope for and certain of what we do not see.

Find a way to take a risk for God today.

❧ God's Attributes

He Is Spirit

John 4:23–24: The time is coming and has come when true worshippers will worship the Father in Spirit and in Truth, for *God is Spirit,* and His worshippers must worship in Spirit and in Truth.

He Gives Us His Spirit

I Corinthians 3:16: Do you not know that you are the temple of God, and that the Spirit of God dwells in you.

Acknowledge His presence in you, and ask Him to fill you now.

He Is Strong

Psalm 24:3: Who is the King of Glory? The Lord, strong and mighty, He is the king of glory.

He Gives Us His Strength

Isaiah 40:31: They that wait upon the Lord shall renew their strength. They shall mount up with wings as eagles. They shall run and not be weary. They shall walk and not faint.

Decide to stand on that promise today.

He Is Faithful

Numbers 23:19: God is not man that He should lie, nor a son of man that He should repent. Has He said, and will He not do it? Has He spoken, and will He not make it good?

He Is Faithful To Us

Lamentations 3:22–23: The Lord's loving kindnesses indeed never cease, for His compassions never fail. They are new every morning; great is Thy faithfulness.

List the areas of your life where God has proved his faithfulness. Give thanks to Him. Speak words of praise for what He has done in you.

God's Resources ❧

In preparation for worship, silently answer the following multiple-choice question.

Living for God is:
- a) A joy
- b) An unpleasant necessity
- c) A ball-and-chain

HIS SPIRIT
I Corinthians 3:16: You have received not the spirit of the world, but the Spirit Who is from God, so that you may know the things freely given us by God.

Call upon His Spirit now to enable you to fellowship with the Living God.

HIS STRENGTH
Philippians 4:13: I can do all things through Christ, Who strengthens me.

Say that out loud several times, each time emphasizing another word.

i.e.: *I* can do all things through Christ…

I *can* do all things through Christ…

HIS FAITHFULNESS
Lamentations 3:22–23: The steadfast love of the Lord never fails for His mercies never come to an end. They are new every morning; great is Thy faithfulness.

"Lord, your steadfast love never fails. That's what I want to count on today. That's what I want to reflect to my world. I fling myself upon your mercies, which never come to an end. Hallelujah! I know some people who need this news. Please bring opportunity to share today."

❦ A Glimpse Of Heavenly Worship

He Is Alpha And Omega

Revelation 1:8: "I am the Alpha and the Omega," says the Lord God, "who is, and who was, and who is to come, the Almighty."

God exists outside all categories. He does not submit to reason. One cannot think Him down to a definition or philosophy. Only He is self-existent. Stop now and abandon, yield, surrender, and relinquish yourself to Him.

He Is Holy

Revelation 4:6, 8: In the center, around the throne, were four living creatures…Day and night they never stop saying: "Holy, holy, holy is the Lord God Almighty, who was, and is, and is to come."

"God, Your holiness is more uninterrupted than the Sahara Desert. Your holiness is more vast and uncharted than unknown galaxies. It is brighter and more constant than a polar summer. Your holiness is less affected by circumstance than a woman who is in labor. Your holiness is purer than a drink of the purest water from the purest river from the purest snow ever to fall on the newly created earth."

He Is Worthy

Revelation 4:10–11: The twenty-four elders fall down before him who sits on the throne, and worship him who lives for ever and ever. They lay their crowns before the throne and say: "You are worthy, our Lord and God, to receive glory and honor and power, for you created all things."

Lay every compliment and every accomplishment at the feet of Christ.…Then pray this prayer out loud: You are worthy…

Living Water ❦

John 4:14: "Whoever drinks the water I give him will never thirst. Indeed, the water I give him will become in him a spring of water welling up to eternal life."

Living Water Received
John 4:10: "If you knew the gift of God and who it is that asks you for a drink, you would have asked him and he would have given you living water."

"Dear Lord Jesus, You have given me new life, and I welcome You today. Be with me, and reveal Yourself to me. Hallelujah!"

Living Water Released
John 7:38–39: "Whoever believes in me, as the Scripture has said, streams of living water will flow from within him." By this he meant the Spirit.

Is this living water flowing out in the midst of my daily living as I love, witness to, reconcile, and encourage others? "Lord, use me as a fountain to splash your forgiveness and acceptance on others."

Living Water Returned
Ephesians 5:18–20: Be filled with the Spirit. Speak to one another with psalms, hymns and spiritual songs. Sing and make music in your heart to the Lord, always giving thanks to God the Father for everything, in the name of our Lord Jesus Christ.

This living water continually fills us, and returns to its source as we worship. Turn your watch upside down, and every time you glance at it today, let it remind you to give thanks to God.

 Mercy

MERCIFUL GOD

Hosea 11:8–9: How can I give you up? How can I hand you over? How can I treat you like the cities I have destroyed? My heart is changed within me; all my compassion is aroused. I will not carry out my fierce anger, nor will I turn and devastate you. For I am God, and not man—the Holy One among you. I will not come in wrath.

Lift your heart in praise to a merciful God.

MERCIFUL CHRIST

Titus 3:5: He saved us, not according to deeds which we have done in righteousness, but according to His *mercy.*

I Peter 1:3: Praise be to the God and Father of our Lord Jesus Christ! In His great *mercy* He has given us new birth.

Kyrie eleison; Christe eleison! Lord have mercy; Christ have mercy! Acknowledge the undeserved favor you have received.

MERCIFUL ME

Micah 6:8: He has showed you, O man, what is good. And what does the Lord require of you? To do justice, *to love mercy,* and to walk humbly with your God.

"Dear Lord, I confess that I have not loved mercy; I have loved vengeance. I have slapped the other cheek, rather than turning it. I have given less, not more, than was asked. I have done unto others before they could do unto me. I have loved only my friends and have treated my enemies with contempt. I know that accepting Your mercy requires that I show some of my own, but I come up short in this area. Change my heart, O God."

The "Omni's" ❦

Based On Observations By Tozer

OMNISCIENCE

"God knows instantly and effortlessly all matter and all matters. Because God knows all things perfectly, He knows nothing better than any other thing. He never discovers anything, He is never surprised, never amazed. He never wonders about anything, nor does He seek information or ask questions."

(Knowledge of the Holy, pg. 62–63)

"Lord, when I think about Your omniscience, I feel terror that You know my secret sins and impure motivations. I also feel a fascination that you would call me to yourself with the full knowledge of everything I am, have been, and will be."

OMNIPOTENCE

Jeremiah 32:17: Ah Lord God, Thou hast made the heavens and the earth by Thy great power. Nothing is too difficult for Thee.

Nothing is too hard for God; nothing is outside His control. Silently speak your impossible situations, your unconquerable addictions, your unreachable acquaintances to the God Who can do anything.

OMNIPRESENCE

Psalm 139:9–10: If I rise on the wings of the dawn, if I settle on the far side of the sea, even there your hand will guide me, your right hand will hold me fast.

Omnipresence means that we can't run away from God; nor do we have to go find Him. Acknowledge his presence and his closeness to you now. Picture Him next to you, and with you in all the situations you will be in today. Look back over these three "Omni's" and speak words of praise to this great God.

❦ Pictures Of God

Read of these Biblical descriptions of God and allow your heart to be in awe of Him!

Creator God
Psalm 24:1: The Earth is the Lord's and everything in it. The world and all who dwell in it. For He founded it upon the seas and established it upon the waters. *God is a Creator God!*

Almighty God
Jeremiah 32:17: Ah Lord God, Thou hast made the heavens and the earth by Thy great power. Nothing is too difficult for Thee. *God is an Almighty God!*

All-Knowing God
Psalm 139:1–4: O Lord, you have searched me and you know me. You know when I sit and when I rise. You perceive my thoughts from afar. You know my going out and my lying down. You are familiar with all my ways. Before a word is on my tongue, You know it completely. *God is an All-Knowing God!*

Ever-Present God
Psalm 139: 7–10: Where can I go from your Spirit? If I take the wings of the morning and dwell in the uttermost parts of the sea, even there Your hand will lead me and Your right hand will hold me. *God is an Ever-Present God!*

Unchanging God
Malachi 3:6: I the Lord do not change. *God is Immutable!*

Kneel and worship Him as Creator; Almighty; All-Knowing; Ever-Present; Immutable (Unchanging)!

Repentant Fruit ❦

Luke 3:8: Produce fruit in keeping with repentance.

How does *repentance* affect or mutate the fruit of the Spirit? Is repentance the orchard in which the fruit grows? Is it the fertilizer? Does repentance provide the right motive for the right action? How do a repentant person's definitions of the fruit of the Spirit differ from the average? What does repentant fruit look like?

Repentant Love—When a recipient of undeserved love is impelled to give that love to an undeserving person.

Repentant Joy—Gratitude provoked by forgiveness. Freedom mixed with relief.

Repentant Peace—The realization that your inability to earn salvation is equal to your ability to un-earn it.

Repentant Patience—When the memories of you at your worst cause you to wait for others to be at their best.

Repentant Kindness—When self-inflicted scars incite care for the self-inflicted wounds of the self-indulgent.

Repentant Goodness—The sense that "repentant kindness" is both privilege and responsibility.

Repentant Faithfulness—When the commitment to faithfulness is fueled by its benefactor.

Repentant Gentleness—How one quadriplegic would feed another quadriplegic, if they could move their hands.

Repentant Self-control—When strength and weakness are out for a drive together, and the signal is always yellow.

❧ Sovereignty

All-Knowing
Psalms 139:1–2: O God you have searched me and you know me. You know when I sit and when I rise; you perceive my thoughts from afar.

If God knows everything, then nothing is unforeseen; there are no accidents. Does this make you angry? Satisfied? Hopeless? Content? Tell God your feelings.

All-Powerful
Jeremiah 32:17: Ah Sovereign Lord, you have made the heavens and the earth by your great power and outstretched arm. Nothing is too hard for you.

If there exists one ounce of power that God doesn't have, then someone else has it, and His rule is limited. However, He can do anything! Think of "impossible" people to reach for Christ and pray for them in faith, believing God can do anything.

Sovereign
Jeremiah 27:5: This is what the Lord Almighty, the God of Israel, says: "Tell this to your masters: With my great power and outstretched arm I made the earth and its people and the animals that are on it, and I give it to anyone I please."

He knows everything and can do anything. This is called Sovereignty, and is the attribute by which He rules the world. Lift your hands to the Sovereign Lord and pray:

"No one is higher than The Highest!
    No one is mightier than The Almighty!
        No one is older than The Eternal!
No one is wiser than The All-wise God!
    No one is more powerful than The King!
        No one understands more than The Creator!"

The Gospel #1 ❦

God's plan of salvation begins with Himself.

God Is Awesome And Holy

Exodus 15:11: Who is like you, O Lord—majestic in holiness, awesome in glory, working wonders?

Celebrate God as Awesome and Holy.

Sin Separates

God's plan continues with a requirement.

Leviticus 11:44: Be holy, because I am holy.

The problem is that all of us have sinned (Romans 3:23), and that sin causes both death (Romans 6:23) and separation from God. Take some silent moments and confess your sins to the Lord.

Christ The Bridge

Good news! Death and separation are not for us!

Romans 5:8: God shows His love for us in that, while we were yet sinners, Christ died for us.

This is why I am to rejoice! He has rebuilt the bridge between a holy God and a sinful person.

Changed

II Corinthians 5:17: If anyone is in Christ, they are a new creation.

"Lord, I confess that when I look in the mirror I don't see a new creation. And if I were to ask my friends, I'm not sure they would, either. Continue your life-changing work in me, even when I ask you to stop. I am yours."

❦ The Gospel #2

God Loves People

Hebrews 13:5: I will never fail you nor forsake you.

John 10:10: I have come that they might have life, and have it abundantly.

"Why you love me, Lord, I don't understand. Still, I am so grateful for your love that I want to bathe in this truth always. Thank You."

Sin Separates

Romans 3:23: All have sinned and fallen short of the glory of God.

Confess your sins silently to the Lord.

Christ Reconciles

I Peter 3:18: Christ died for sins, once for all, the just for the unjust, in order that He might bring us to God.

God's great love has found a way to satisfy my offenses. Jesus Christ has joined together what my sin had separated. Praise Him!

I Am Changed

II Corinthians 5:17: If anyone is in Christ he is a new creation.

Hallelujah! This Savior, this Christ, has accomplished more than bringing us to God; He has actually changed our very nature. Speak out loud this praise to God.

Psalm 103:1–4: Bless the Lord, O my soul, and all that is within me bless His holy Name. Bless the Lord, O my soul, and forget not all His benefits—who forgives all your sins, and heals your diseases, who redeems your life from the pit and crowns you with love and compassion.

Ephesians 1—The Trinity ✵

Father
Verses 3–6: Praise be to the God and Father of our Lord Jesus Christ, who has blessed us in the heavenly realms with every spiritual blessing in Christ. For he chose us in him before the creation of the world to be holy and blameless in his sight. In love he predestined us to be adopted as his sons through Jesus Christ, in accordance with his pleasure and will—to the praise of his glorious grace which he has freely given us in the One he loves.

Meditate on the work of the Father: He blessed us; He chose us; He adopted us; He gave us grace.

Son
Verses 7–8: In him we have redemption through his blood, the forgiveness of sins, in accordance with the riches of God's grace that he lavished on us with all wisdom and understanding.

Meditate on the work of the Son: He redeems us; He forgives us; He lavishes grace upon us.

Holy Spirit
Verses 13–14: And you also were included in Christ when you heard the word of truth, the gospel of your salvation. Having believed, you were marked in him with a seal, the promised Holy Spirit, who is a deposit guaranteeing our inheritance until the redemption of those who are God's possession—to the praise of his glory.

"Lord, I do not understand You, but I worship You. I give thanks for the Holy Spirit who shows me Christ. I give praise for Jesus who shows me the Father. I worship the Father who gives me His Spirit. I do not understand You, but I worship You. Hallelujah!"

❧ A Meditation On "What A Friend We Have In Jesus"

Give Him Your Guilt
"What a friend we have in Jesus
  All our sins and griefs to bear!
What a privilege to carry
  Everything to God in prayer!
O what peace we often forfeit
  O what needless pain we bear
All because we do not carry
  Everything to God in prayer!"

I Peter 3:18: Christ died for sins once for all, the righteous for the unrighteous, to bring you to God. He was put to death in the body but made alive by the Spirit.

Psalm 51:17: The sacrifices of God are a broken spirit; a broken and contrite heart, O God, you will not despise.

Silently confess your sins to the Lord.

Give Him Your Discouragement
"Have we trials and temptations?
  Is there trouble anywhere?
We should never be discouraged,
  Take it to the Lord in Prayer!
Can we find a friend so faithful,
  Who will all our sorrows share?
Jesus knows our every weakness,
  Take it to the Lord in prayer!"

Hebrews 2:18: Because he himself suffered when he was tempted, he is able to help those who are being tempted.

Like the Apostle Paul, we sometimes do the very thing we don't want to do. Weakness is demoralizing. Give Him any discouragement you might be feeling.

Give Him Your Anxieties

"Are we weak and heavy laden
  Cumbered with a load of care?
Precious Savior, still our refuge
  Take it to the Lord in prayer!
Do thy friends despise, forsake thee?
  Take it to the Lord in Prayer!
In His arms He'll take and shield thee
  Thou wilt find a solace there."

Isaiah 41:10: Do not fear, for I am with you; do not be dismayed, for I am your God. I will strengthen you and help you; I will uphold you with my righteous right hand.

Sometimes we are afraid. Sometimes people hurt us, and we are left holding the bag. Christ calls us to give our "bag of hurts and worries" to Him. Do that now.

 The Word Reveals God

God has given us His Word, the Holy Bible, enabling us to know certain aspects of His character.

He Is Faithful

Lamentations 3:22–23: The Lord's loving kindnesses never cease; His compassions never fail; they are new each morning; great is Thy Faithfulness!

Acknowledge His faithfulness with your words of thanks.

His Name Is Great

Philippians 2:9: God has bestowed upon Christ a name that is above all names, that at the name of Jesus every knee should bow in heaven and on earth and under the earth, and every tongue confess that Jesus Christ is Lord, to the glory of God the Father.

As a praise to God, list as many of his names as possible.

He Is Exalted

Psalm 108:5: Be exalted, O God, above the heavens, and let your glory be over all the earth.

Think of some of the ways He is exalted.
    "Lord, You are exalted above _____."

He Is Worthy

Revelation 4:11: Thou art worthy, O Lord, to receive glory and honor and power, for thou has created all things.

"Holy, Holy, Holy Lord. God of power and might. Heaven and earth are filled with Your glory. Hosanna in the highest. Blessed is He who comes in the name of the Lord. Hosanna in the highest."

PATHWAY

 A.C.T.S.

Psalm 113 commands all *servants* of the Lord to *praise the* name *of the Lord both now and forever more—from the rising of the sun to the place where it sets:* In other words, always and everywhere, not just on Sundays. Use the acronym "A.C.T.S." as one roadmap for your daily worship. A.C.T.S. stands for "Adoration, Confession, Thanksgiving, and Supplication."

ADORATION
Speak out loud some words of adoration, like "O God, You are great. God, You are mighty. You are _____."

Sing or speak: "O Come Let Us Adore Him"

CONFESSION
Take some silent moments to confess your personal sins. (Optional: read Psalm 51 out loud)

THANKSGIVING
List some of the very ordinary things you are thankful for.

Sing or speak: "God Is So Good"

SUPPLICATION
To supplicate is to beseech, to humbly or earnestly ask for. Are there things in your life that you need God to do? Ask Him. Are there people in your life who need His touch? Ask Him. Are there situations which are beyond your control? Ask, that it may be given. Seek, that you may find. Knock, that the door would be opened.

Love God, One Another, And The World

If you were to ask a person "which is the most important commandment?", you might expect to hear "don't steal" or "don't murder." When Christ was asked this question in Matthew 22, He said:

Love God

Verse 37: Love the Lord your God with all your heart and with all your soul and with all your mind.

To take these few moments to worship today is to perform and express the most important commandment ever given. Focus your heart…and your soul…and your mind upon loving God. Take time to speak words of devotion to God. Do not be found guilty of giving half-hearted praise.

Love One Another

Verse 39: The second commandment is like the first: Love your neighbor as yourself.

Ask God if there is any believer with whom you need to reconcile. Though this is hard, it is not more difficult than the results of harboring a grudge.

Love The World

Matthew 28:19: Go and make disciples of all nations.

Christ loves the world, and calls us to do the same. Right now begin praying for those in your life who need the Lord…family members…co-workers…neighbors…enemies.…

# Temple Walk

OUTER COURT

The **Outer Court** was an open and ordinary place. Friends were greeted and daily life was conducted in and around this area. It was the most accessible area of temple worship. List five things that you are thankful for.

INNER COURT

The **Inner Court** was a more somber place. It was a place of sacrifice and death, as the priests offered sacrifices on the altar of God. As you approach the Lord today, remember the death of Christ which purchased your forgiveness, and recognize the need to die to those things which would distract you from your God. Confess your sins to the Lord, and agree with Him about the things in your life which are not acceptable to Him. Pray:

Dear God,

I have worshiped at the altar of my own desires. I have sacrificed much of my time and talent to the god of materialism. Now I stand before your altar, and realize that my desires and strivings for things have crowded out my desire for You. Today I sacrifice the desires of my heart.

HOLY OF HOLIES

The third area of the temple is called the Holy of Holies. Only the High Priest could enter here, and he only once a year, and only after much preparation. This area was separated by a curtain, which we know was torn from top to bottom during the crucifixion of Christ granting passage to all who would approach God appropriately. Come humbly to the Lord, and reverently speak five of His attributes.

Thanks—Praise—Worship ❦

THANKSGIVING
I Thessalonians 5:18: Give thanks in every circumstance; this is the will of God in Christ for you.

We could define "thanksgiving" as *expressing appreciation for the ordinary:* things like family, job, health, education. Perform the will of God by giving Him thanks.

PRAISE
Psalm 113 begins Praise the Lord. Praise, O servants of the Lord. Praise the name of the Lord.

"Praise" might be defined as *expressing appreciation for the specific;* things like forgiveness, hope, acceptance, and courage. *Praise* God for doing in you what you could not do in yourself by speaking out loud the *one word* that describes what God has done for you. For example: "He has _____ me." (i.e. "saved, forgiven, strengthened," etc.)

WORSHIP
I Chronicles 16:29: Worship the Lord in the splendor of his holiness.

When we *worship* God, we express appreciation simply for Who He is, apart from the things He has done.

Silently begin to list the attributes of God: things like "mighty, holy, comforter, provider."

Sing or speak: "I Exalt Thee"

Seasonal

Palm Sunday #1 ❦

RECOGNIZE HIM
Psalm 118:22–24: The stone the builders rejected has become the capstone; the Lord has done this and it is marvelous in our eyes. This is the day the Lord has made; let us rejoice and be glad in it.

This was the *one day* that Christ was recognized as Savior and worshiped as King. Recognize and worship Him now.

ACKNOWLEDGE HIM
Zechariah 9:9: Rejoice greatly, O Daughter of Zion! Shout, Daughter of Jerusalem! See, your king comes to you, righteous and having salvation, gentle and riding on a donkey, on a colt, the foal of a donkey.

Acknowledge Him. Celebrate His actual presence with you.

HONOR HIM
Luke 19:36: As he went along, people spread their cloaks on the road.

John 12:13: They took palm branches and went out to meet him, shouting, "Hosanna!" "Blessed is he who comes in the name of the Lord!" "Blessed is the King of Israel!"

Find a place where you can shout in a loud voice "Hosanna in the highest!" and "Blessed is He who comes in the name of the Lord!"

PRAISE HIM
Luke 19:39–40: Some of the Pharisees in the crowd said to Jesus, "Teacher, rebuke your disciples!" "I tell you," he replied, "If they keep silent, the stones will cry out."

Decide now that you will never be replaced by a rock, and vow to God that you will praise Him until the day you die.

❧ Palm Sunday #2

His Arrival

Imagine the setting of Christ's arrival to Jerusalem in your mind. The landscape is barren; the temperature is hot. Christ and his followers begin to walk toward the City.

John 12:12–13: The great crowd that had come for the Feast heard that Jesus was on his way to Jerusalem. They took palm branches and went out to meet him,

How can we welcome His presence today? Begin speaking out loud your words of thanks to Him. ("thank you for my health; thank you for my job; thank you for…")

His Praise

Verse 13: shouting, "Hosanna!" "Blessed is he who comes in the name of the Lord!" "Blessed is the King of Israel!"

The religious leaders were upset at this turn of events, and asked Jesus to rebuke the people for praising Him. Jesus responded in a way that left no doubt about His identity. He said "I tell you, if they keep quiet, the very rocks will cry out" (Luke 19:40). Speak these phrases (Verse 13) to Christ.

His Cleansing

Matthew 21:12–13: Jesus entered the temple area and drove out all who were buying and selling there. He overturned the tables of the money changers and the benches of those selling doves. "It is written," he said to them, " 'My house will be called a house of prayer,' but you are making it a 'den of robbers.' "

If Christ walked through the temple of your heart, what would offend Him today? What is on the table of your life that He would overturn? What would He drive out with whips? Confess silently to the Lord.

Easter #1 ❦

New Reality
I Corinthians 15:54–55: Death has been swallowed up in victory. Where, O death, is your victory? Where, O death, is your sting?

The proof and truth of the resurrection of Christ changes *reality* as we know it. How has meeting God changed your concept or definition of reality and truth.

New Life
II Timothy 1:9–10: This grace was given us in Christ Jesus before the beginning of time, but it has now been revealed through the appearing of our Savior, Christ Jesus, who has *destroyed death* and has *brought life* and immortality to light through the gospel.

The proof and truth of the resurrection of Christ also changes *life* as we know it. How has meeting God changed your life? Give God thanks for the new life which is yours in Christ!

New Hope
I John 3:3: What we will be has not yet been made known. But we know that when he appears, we shall be like him, for we shall see him as he is. Everyone who has this hope in him purifies himself, just as he is pure.

Revelation 21:4: He will wipe every tear from their eyes. There will be no more death or mourning or crying or pain, for the old order of things has passed away.

Finally, the proof and truth of the resurrection of Christ gives us hope, both in this life, and beyond the grave. How has meeting God changed your view of death? Give Him praise.

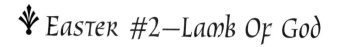 Easter #2—Lamb Of God

Passover Lamb

Exodus 12:23: When the Lord goes through the land to strike down the Egyptians, he will see the blood on the top and sides of the door frame and will pass over that doorway, and he will not permit the destroyer to enter your houses and strike you down.

Take a moment to thank God for the many troubles which have "passed over" you because of knowing Christ.

Lamb Of God

In John 1:29, John the Baptizer sees Jesus and says, Look, the Lamb of God, who takes away the sin of the world!

Lambs were meant for sacrifice, and John knew that this time the blood would be spread upon a cross instead of a doorpost. Take time to silently praise Him for the forgiveness that is yours.

Risen, Living Lamb

Luke 24:1–6: On the first day of the week, very early in the morning, the women took the spices they had prepared and went to the tomb. They found the stone rolled away from the tomb, but when they entered, they did not find the body of the Lord Jesus. In their fright the women bowed down with their faces to the ground, but the men said to them, "Why do you look for the living among the dead? He is not here; he has risen!"

Revelation 1:17–18: Do not be afraid. I am the First and the Last. I am the Living One; I was dead, and behold I am alive for ever and ever!

Say this out loud three times: Where, O death, is your victory? Where, O death, is your sting? (I Corinthians 15:55)

Speak words of gratitude to Him for paying your ransom fee.

Father's Day ❦

Clear Expectations
Psalm 119:105: Thy Word is a lamp unto my feet, and a light unto my path.

Father God has shown us how to live, giving us an owner's manual (Bible) to use. He has promised to guide us through this Word of God. Praise Him for His Word.

Accepting
Father God is so accepting that when Gideon was hiding in a winepress, He called him a mighty man of valor. This Father is so accepting that He chose the stutterer Moses to be His spokesman. This Father chose unrefined and uneducated Peter to preach to the Jews. This Father so accepts us that Romans 5:8 says While we were yet sinners, Christ died for us. Breathe a deep sigh of relief, and praise Him!

Forgiving
Father God is so forgiving that adulterer and murderer David was called a man after God's own heart; Rahab the Gentile harlot was taken to live with the chosen people, and was included in the lineage of Jesus Christ. This Father is so forgiving that He says: I will forget your transgressions, and your sins I will remember no more (Jeremiah 31:34). He says: How can I give you up; how can I hand you over? My heart is changed within me; all my compassion is aroused. I will not carry out my fierce anger (Hosea 11:8–9). Praise Him!

Providing And Caring
Father God is such a provider that in Philippians 4:19 He says: I will supply all your needs. Hebrews 13:5 says: I will never fail nor forsake you. Rest yourself in His arms.

# Patriotic #1

Excerpts from Lincoln's "Gettysburg Address"

> "Fourscore and seven years ago our fathers brought forth upon this continent a new nation, conceived in liberty, and dedicated to the proposition that all men are created equal."

Two millennia ago, God brought forth upon this planet His Son, conceived in purity and dedicated to the task of bringing hope and freedom-of-soul to all mankind.

> "Now we are engaged in a great civil war, testing whether that nation, or any nation so conceived and so dedicated, can long endure. We are met on a great battlefield of that war. We have come to dedicate a portion of that field as a final resting place for those who here gave their lives that nation might live."

Now I am engaged in a great spiritual war, testing whether a redeemed person will continue in newness of life. I trust in *His* name, and remember *His* sacrifice. The gift of His life for me demands a remembrance of Jesus, Who, for the joy set before Him, endured the cross, despising it's shame, and Who is now seated at the right hand of the throne of God.

> "The world will little note nor long remember what we say here; but it can never forget what they did here. It is for us, the living, rather to be dedicated here to the unfinished work which they who fought here have thus far so nobly advanced. It is rather for us to be here dedicated to the great task remaining before us, that from these honored dead we take increased devotion to that cause for which they gave the last full measure of devotion."

I must never forget what Christ has done on my behalf. For just as Jesus was dedicated to the unfinished work of his heavenly Father, giving the last full measure of devotion, so now in heaven He is faithful to me, His child. In this knowledge we press on with every confident hope for all the years and centuries yet to come.

> "...that we here highly resolve that these dead shall not have died in vain; that this nation, under God, shall have a new birth of freedom and that government of the people, by the people, and for the people, shall not perish from the earth."

Resolving that Christ shall not have died in vain, I dedicate myself to live for God's glory, and to communicate to others this new birth of freedom. For I believe and confess that "Christ has died; Christ has risen; Christ will come again."

❧ Patriotic #2—1 Peter 2

We Are Dual Citizens

Verses 16–17: Live as free men, but do not use your freedom as a cover-up for evil; live as servants of God. Show proper respect to everyone: Love the brotherhood of believers, fear God, honor the king.

Express thanks for your freedom, and show proper respect to those who earned that freedom. It is altogether appropriate to honor your heritage.

We Are The People Of God

Verses 9–10: But you are a chosen people, a royal priesthood, a holy nation, a people belonging to God, that you may declare the praises of him who called you out of darkness into his wonderful light. Once you were not a people, but now you are the people of God; once you had not received mercy, but now you have received mercy.

Take time to worship God as a recipient of his mercy should. Recite his deeds and characteristics.

Life Is Temporary

Verse 11: Dear friends, I urge you, as aliens and strangers in the world, to abstain from sinful desires, which war against your soul.

If God went through my garage, home, closet, or schedule, whose kingdom would He think I was building? Commit everything you have and everything you are to the Christ.

Live Well

Verse 12: Live such good lives among the pagans that, though they accuse you of doing wrong, they may see your good deeds and glorify God on the day he visits us.

Pray that the world would see your life and glorify God.

Thanksgiving ❦

Worship Thankfully
Hebrews 12:28: Let us be thankful, and so worship God acceptably with reverence and awe, for our "God is a consuming fire."

Let your mind recall again the amazing life-change which God has performed in you, and let it stimulate your worship.

Speak words of thanks to God.

Speak words of worship with reverence and awe.

Act Thankfully
I Thessalonians 5:18: Give thanks in all circumstances, for this is the will of God in Christ for you.

We might be thankful *because of* our circumstances, or we might have to be thankful *in spite of* our circumstances. The command is to be thankful, so, picture each circumstance of your life; financial, relationship, vocation, health, etc., and cause yourself to give thanks to God.

Pray Thankfully
Philippians 4:6: Do not be anxious about anything, but in everything, by prayer and supplication, with thanksgiving, present your requests to God.

One by one, silently present your specific requests to God. After each request, thank God in faith for the way He will answer.

Sing Thankfully
Psalm 28:7: And I will give thanks to him in song.

Decided to give thanks every hour on the hour for the things you normally take for granted. Sing or speak the words to the song "Give Thanks."

 *Advent*

Prophecy
Read Isaiah 9:2–7

The Scriptures remind us that the prophets of God predicted and expected the coming of the Messiah. Silently welcome Christ.

Bethlehem
Read Matthew 2:1–6

The Scriptures remind us that Christ was born as a human baby in a specific place and at a specific time in history. Acknowledge His desire to be born in you, and invite Him again to reside in all the circumstances of your life.

Shepherds
Read Luke 2:8–12, 16–18

The Scriptures tell us that the shepherds shared the joy of Christ's birth as they knelt in worship before the manger. Bow yourself before Christ.

Angels
Read Luke 2:8–14

The Scriptures say that the angels sang as they proclaimed the glory of Christ's birth to the shepherds. Offer a song or words of glory to the King.

Christ
Read Matthew 1:18–25

Christ is present in our world. Christ is born! Rejoice in Him by speaking words of gratitude for what He has done in you.

Shepherds—Luke 2 ❦

WAIT-WATCHING

Verse 8: And there were shepherds living out in the fields nearby, keeping watch over their flocks at night.

The Shepherds had been waiting for Messiah like their fathers before them and their fathers before them. "Lord, let me long for Your return as these longed for your coming."

GOOD NEWS

Verses 9–11: An angel of the Lord appeared to them, and the glory of the Lord shone around them, and they were terrified. But the angel said to them, "Do no be afraid. I bring you good news of great joy that will be for all the people. Today in the town of David a Savior has been born to you; he is Christ the Lord."

The Shepherds are suddenly confronted with the news that generations have longed to hear. Think back to when and where you first heard the good news.

SEEK CHRIST

Verse 15: When the angels had left them and gone into heaven, the shepherds said to one another, "Let's go to Bethlehem and see this thing that has happened, which the Lord has told us about."

The shepherds dropped everything to go and find Christ. What is it that would keep you from finding Him today? Set those things aside. Seek Christ.

WORSHIP HIM

Verse 17 simply says that the shepherds saw the child. We don't know much of what they did there, but they must have looked on the child; they must have bowed before Him. Imagine the thoughts and feelings you would have had kneeling before that manger. Speak those to Christ now.

 Christmas Eve Meditation

*Excerpts from St. Augustine's Christmas Sermons

CHRIST IS BORN

John 1:1,14: In the beginning was the Word, and the Word was *with* God, and the Word *was* God....And the Word became flesh and dwelt among us.

INTO TIME

*He, through whom time was made, was made in time.

He, older by eternity than the world itself, became younger in age than His servants.

He was born of a father as God and of a mother as man.

One is without time, the other without parallel.

INTO FLESH

*He who made man, was made man.

He was given existence by a mother who He brought into existence.

He nursed at the breasts which He filled.

INTO SUBMISSION

*He was carried in the hands which He had formed.

He cried like a babe in speechless infancy,

This Word without whom human eloquence is speechless.

The Truth is accused by false witnesses.

The Judge of the living and the dead is judged by mortals.

The Teacher is beaten by the student.

The Vine is crowned with thorns.

INTO HEARTS

*Who, then, shall declare His generation?

Let us in His presence try to realize the abasement that He in all His majesty accepted for our sakes. And let us be kindled with love, that we may come to His eternity.

APPENDICES

How-To's

Thanksgiving
Choose an area of your life and thank God
    for everything in it; be specific.
Look around; thank God for what you see.

Humility
Compare and contrast.
    (You are great, I am small; etc.)
What would life be like if you hadn't met God?

Surrender
Go through each arena of your life (home, work, hobbies, etc.),
    surrendering each as you do.
Go through your checkbook and surrender each thing to God.

Adoration
Attributes; Names; Combine Names and Attributes.
Flip through Psalms and speak phrases of praise.

Assurances
List the assurances you know are scriptural.
Read/recite a creed.
Write your own Biblically-based creed.

Promises
Picture Christ speaking a promise directly to you.
Review promises that have been important to you.

Resources
List the things God has provided to help you obey.
Think on the things God has that you don't.

Names of God

YAWEH
(I AM)

YAWEH-Jireh
(The Lord our Provider)

YAWEH-Nissi
(The Lord our Banner)

YAWEH-Shalom
(The Lord our Peace)

YAWEH-Tsidkenu
(The Lord our Righteousness)

YAWEH-Rohi
(The Lord our Shepherd)

YAWEH-M'kaddes
(The Lord Who Sanctifies)

YAWEH-Rophe
(The Lord our Healer)

YAWEH-Shammah
(The Lord is Present)

EL ELYON
(The Lord Most High)

Resources and Promises

HIS LOVE
Jn. 10:10
Ps. 103:8–13

HIS PRESENCE
Heb. 13:5
Deut. 31:6

SALVATION
I Jn. 5:11–13
Rom. 8:1

ANSWERED PRAYER
Jn. 16:24
Ps. 37:4
Ps. 120:1

VICTORY
I Cor. 10:13
Phil. 4:19

HIS GUIDANCE
Prov. 3:5–6
Isa. 30:21
Ps. 143:8

FORGIVENESS
I Jn. 1:9
Ps. 103:12

HIS SPIRIT
I Cor. 3:16
I Cor. 2:12

HIS FAITHFULNESS
Num. 23:19
Lam. 3:22
Ps. 27:13–14
Ps. 66:20

HIS STRENGTH
Isa. 41:10

HIS PEACE
Isa. 26:3
I Pet. 5:7

HIS PROTECTION
Isa. 43:1–3a

HIS PROVISION
Rom. 8:32
Phil. 4:13

HIS HELP IN TEMPTATION
Heb. 2:18
Ps. 119:9–11
II Sam. 33:31–34

HIS COMFORT
Jn. 14:1

HEAVEN
Jn. 14:2–3

Titles and Descriptions of God

A
Advocate
Almighty God
Alpha and Omega
Author and Finisher of our
    Faith

B
Beautiful
Beginning and the End
Beloved of the Father
Bishop of our Souls
Bread of Life
Bridegroom
Bright and Morning Star

C
Comforter
Cornerstone
Creator

D
Defender
Deliverer
Desire of Nations
Door

E
Eternal Life
Everlasting Father

F
Faithful and
    True Witness
Firstborn
Fortress
Friend

G
Gate
God
Good Shepherd
Governor
Guardian

H
Head of the Church
Healer
Helper
Holy
Holy One of Israel

I
I AM
Image of the Invisible God
Immanuel
Immortal
Inheritance

J
Jesus of Nazareth
Judge
Justifier

K
King Eternal
King of Glory
King of Israel
King of Kings
King of the Jews

L
Lamb of God
Life
Light of Men

Titles and Descriptions of God

Light of the World
Lily of the Valley
Lion of the
    Tribe of Judah
Lord of Lords
Lord God Almighty
Lord Jesus Christ

M
Maker
Man of Sorrows
Master
Mediator
Merciful
Messiah
Mighty God

N
Name Above all Names
Nazarene

O
One with the Father
Only Begotten of the Father
Only Wise God

P
Pearl of Great Price
Physician
Priest
Prince of Peace

R
Rabbi
Redeemer
Refuge
Resurrection and the Life

Righteous Judge
Rock of Salvation
Rose of Sharon

S
Savior
Shepherd
Shield
Son of Man
Son of the Living God
Stone the Builders Rejected
Strength
Suffering Servant
Sun of Righteousness
Sure Foundation

T
Teacher
Truth

U
Undefiled

V
Very Present Help
Vine

W
Way
Wonderful Counselor
Word of God
Word of Life
Worthy

Attributes of God

Taken from *Knowledge of the Holy* by A.W. Tozer. Adapted

ETERNAL
(dwells outside time)

FAITHFUL
(perfectly/completely
consistent)

GOOD
(nature is to bless)

GRACIOUS
(bestows benefit on the
undeserving)

HOLY
(infinite, incomprehensible
fullness of purity)

IMMUTABLE
(changeless and consistent)

INFINITE
(limitless, boundless,
measureless)

JUST
(confronts moral inequity)

LOVING
(wills the good of all)

MERCIFUL
(reaction to suffering and
guilt)

OMNIPOTENT
(having all power)

OMNIPRESENT
(universally next to)

OMNISCIENCE
(complete knowledge)

SELF-EXISTENT
(no origin)

SELF-SUFFICIENT
(contains all)

SOVEREIGN
(rules with complete freedom)

TRANSCENDENT
(unimaginable)

TRIUNE
(three-in-one; one-in-three)

ALL-WISE
(devise/achieve perfect ends by
perfect means)

Nicene Creed

I believe in one God the Father Almighty, Maker of heaven and earth, and of all things visible and invisible:
And in one Lord Jesus Christ, the only-begotten Son of God, begotten of His Father before all worlds, God of God, Light of Light, very God of very God, begotten, not made, being of one substance with the Father, by whom all things were made;

Who for us men and for our salvation came down from heaven, and was incarnate by the Holy Spirit of the Virgin Mary, and was made man, and crucified also for us under Pontius Pilate;

He suffered and was buried, and the third day He rose again according to the Scriptures, and ascended into heaven, and sitteth on the right hand of the Father;

And He shall come again with glory to judge both the quick and the dead;

Whose Kingdom shall have no end.

And I believe in the Holy Spirit, the Lord and Giver of life, who proceedeth from the Father and the Son, who with the Father and the Son together is worshiped and glorified; who spoke by the prophets. And I believe in one catholic and apostolic church; I acknowledge one baptism for the remission of sins, and I look for the resurrection of the dead, and the life of the world to come. Amen.

A Contemporary Affirmation of Faith
from the *WORD Hymnal*, p. 663

I believe in Jesus Christ the Lord, Who was promised to the people of Israel, Who came in the flesh to dwell among us, Who announced the coming of the rule of God, Who gathered disciples and taught them, Who died on the cross to free us from sin, Who rose from the dead to give us life and hope, Who reigns in heaven at the right hand of God, Who comes to judge and bring justice to victory.

I believe in God His Father, Who raised Him from the dead, Who created and sustains the universe, Who acts to deliver His people in times of need, Who desires all men everywhere to be saved, Who rules over the destinies of men and nations, Who continues to love men even when they reject Him.

I believe in the Holy Spirit, Who is the form of God present in the church, Who moves men to faith and obedience, Who is the guarantee of our deliverance, Who leads us to find God's will in the Word, Who assists those whom He renews in prayer, Who guides us in discernment, Who impels us to act together.

I believe He made us His people, to invite others to follow Christ, to encourage one another to deeper commitment, to proclaim forgiveness of sins and hope, to reconcile men to God through word and deed, to bear witness to the power of love over hate, to proclaim Jesus the Lord over all, to meet the daily tasks of life with purpose, to suffer joyfully for the cause of right, to the ends of the earth, to the end of the age, to the praise of His glory. Amen.

Apostles' Creed

I believe in God the Father Almighty, maker of heaven and earth:

And in Jesus Christ His only Son, our Lord; who was conceived by the Holy Spirit, born of the Virgin Mary, suffered under Pontius Pilate, was crucified, dead, and buried; He descended into Hades; the third day He rose again from the dead; He ascended into heaven, and sitteth on the right hand of God, the Father Almighty; from thence He shall come to judge the quick and the dead.

I believe in the Holy Spirit, the holy catholic church, the communion of saints, the forgiveness of sins, the resurrection of the body, and the life everlasting. Amen.

THE PRACTICE OF THE PRESENCE OF GOD

BY BROTHER LAWRENCE

[ADAPTED, CATEGORIZED, PERSONALIZED]

On the Priority of His Presence

Continually establish myself in a sense of God's presence by continually conversing with Him.

Apply myself with diligence to form a habit of conversing with God continually, referring all I do to Him.

My only business is to love and delight myself in God.

Accustom myself to a continual conversation with Him, with freedom and in simplicity.

Walk before God simply, in faith, with humility and with love.

Apply myself diligently to do nothing and think nothing which may displease Him.

Persevere in His holy presence.

Keep an habitual, silent, and secret conversation of the soul with God.

God has infinite treasure to bestow. He pours His graces and favors plentifully; they flow like a torrent. But I often stop this torrent by the little value I set upon it.

Let me make way for grace.

Let me redeem the lost time.

Always work at it, because not to advance in the spiritual life is to go back.

There is not in the world a kind of life more sweet and delightful than that of a continual conversation with God.

Continue with Him my commerce of love, persevering in His holy presence, one while by an act of praise, of adoration, or of desire; one while by an act of resignation or thanksgiving; and in all the ways which my spirit can invent.

He requires no great matters of me: a little remembrance of Him from time to time; a little adoration; sometimes to pray for His grace, sometimes to offer Him my sufferings, and sometimes to return Him thanks for the favors He has given me, and still gives me, in the midst of my troubles, and to console myself with Him the oftenest I can.

Lift up my heart to Him, sometimes at meals, and when I am in company; the least little remembrance will always be acceptable to Him. I need not cry very loud; He is nearer to me than I am aware of.

Do not always scrupulously confine myself to certain rules, or particular forms of devotion, but act with a general confidence in God, with love and humility.

Let it be my business to keep my mind in the presence of the Lord.

One way to recollect the mind easily at prayer time is not to let it wander too far at other times.My only business in this life is to please God.

A holy habit: to think of Him always.

I must know before I can love. In order to know God, I must often think of Him; and when I come to love Him, I shall also think of Him often, for my heart will be with my treasure.

Love others, but without encroaching upon the love due to God.

If I would enjoy the peace of paradise in this life I must accustom myself to a familiar, humble, affectionate conversation with Him.

I must hinder my spirit's wandering from Him upon any occasion.

Watch continually over myself, that I may not do nor say nor think anything that may displease Him.

To arrive at this state, the beginning is difficult, for I must act purely in faith.

Let all my employment be to know God.

Do not love God merely for His favors, for they cannot bring me as near to God as one simple act of faith. Let me seek Him often by faith.

On The Practice Of His Presence

Nourish my soul with high notions of God.

I cannot do good unless You enable me.

Act with God in great simplicity, speaking to Him frankly and plainly, imploring His assistance in all affairs as they happen.

Do everything for the love of God, and with prayer, upon all occasions.

Reject useless thoughts as soon as they are perceived.

Desire only that I might not offend Him.

Perform all actions for the love of God.

Consider myself as a poor criminal at the feet of his judge.

Behold Him in my heart as a Father.

Drive from my mind everything that is capable of interrupting my thought of God.

Consider myself as a stone before a carver.

Let my soul ascend and continue as it were suspended and firmly fixed in God, as in its center and place of rest.

"My God, here I am all devoted to Thee. Lord, make me according to Thy heart."

If the vessel of my soul is tossed with winds and storms, awake the Lord, who rests in it, and He will quickly calm the sea.

On Work
Brother Lawrence's Work Prayer

> "O my God,
>   Since You are with me always
>   And since my responsibilities require me to apply my
>   mind to these outward things
>   I beg You to grant me the grace
>   To continue in Your presence.
>   Please assist me in this
>   And receive all my works
>   And possess all my affections."

Never hasty nor loitering; do each thing in its season, with an even, uninterrupted composure and tranquillity of spirit.

Worship Him, beg His grace, offer Him my heart, even in the midst of my daily business.

Most excellent method of going to God is that of doing our common business without any view of pleasing men; purely for the love of God.

On Sufferings
Sufferings will be sweet and pleasant to me while I am with Him; and the greatest pleasures will be, without Him, a cruel punishment to me.

Happy those who suffer with Him. Suffer in that manner, and seek from Him the strength to endure as much, and as long, as He shall judge to be necessary for you.

Don't consider sickness as a pain from nature, but rather, a favor of God.

Find in suffering great sweetness and sensible consolation.

He often sends diseases of the body to cure those of the soul.

Be satisfied with the condition in which God places me.

Offer Him my pains incessantly; pray to Him for strength to endure them.

Get a habit of entertaining myself often with God, forgetting Him the least I can. Adore Him in my infirmities, offering myself to Him from time to time, and in the height of my sufferings beseech Him humbly and affectionately.

Ask of God not deliverance from my pains, but strength to bear resolutely, for the love of Him, all that He should please, and as long as He shall please.

He is the Father of the afflicted.

However great the sufferings may be, receive them with love.

If I knew how much He loves me, I should always be ready to receive equally and with indifference from His hand the sweet and the bitter.

When I see afflictions as dispensed by the hand of my loving Father, my sufferings will lose their bitterness and become matters of consolation.

On Other Things

God always gives light in my doubts when I have no other designs but to please Him.

Sanctification does not depend upon changing my works, but in doing that for God's sake which I commonly do for my own.

Don't weary of doing little things for the love of God, who regards not the greatness of the work, but the love with which it is performed.

The best goal to set is to become the most perfect worshiper of God I can possibly be.

The greater perfection a soul aspires after, the more dependent it is upon divine grace.

Don't go faster than grace. One does not become holy all at once.

If He left me one moment to myself I should be the most wretched man alive.

Worship Leading Resources

Worship

A Seven Week Church Curriculum teaching and applying the concepts of worship

Includes:
Teaching outlines, transparency masters, class handouts.

Worship: What is it?	Why Worship?
Relationship Participants	Thinking of God
Renewal in Worship	In Spirit and in Truth
To Worship the Almighty	

$19.95

Ten Essays On Worship
Christian Worship and Music: Philosophies, Analogies, Practicalities

Look, Ma, No Congregation	Religion or Relationship
To Appreciate The Almighty	Keeping The Love Alive
Can I Play, Too?	The Word In Worship
Worship = Singing?	Leading Gently Forward
Instrumental Music Vocations	To Frame a Song

$14.95

Roadmaps™ For Blended Worship
Self-contained, Twelve-minute Worship Packages
Incorporating the great Hymns with the best Scripture Songs

Volumes 1, 2, 3. 4
Each contains 16 worship packages

A Balanced Use of Hymns and Scripture Songs
Verbal Introductions and Transitions

From Sound & Light Music

Keyboard References
Keys and Clues
Songslide Selections and References

$19.95

CONFESSIONS OF A CHRISTIAN MUSICIAN
Prayers of Confession & Poems of Surrender

For professional musicians who struggle with their faith.
For church musicians who struggle with their art.
For worship leaders who struggle with their priorities.

$9.95

ROADMAPS™ FOR TRADITIONAL WORSHIP
Twenty Inspiring Calls to Worship with Optional Hymn Selections

Short Meditations which Focus the Worshiper and provide
Frames of Reference for Traditional Hymns

$14.95

MEDITATIONS OF A CHRISTIAN MUSICIAN
Reflections on a Lifestyle of Holiness
If we are too busy to think, we end up with life, but no style!

December Lives for June Living	Legalism—The Great Thief
Ponderings & Proverbs	Unspiritual Gifts
Of Fathers and Sons	Much more!

$9.95

IVORY AND BRASS RECORDINGS

Couldn't Help Myself
Sacred instrumental solos that kick

God's Love 'N' Lullabies
Traditional and original Christian lullabies

An Ivory and Brass Christmas
Hip Christmas arrangements for trumpet and piano

Deja New
Instrumental renditions of Classics and early American songs

All Cassettes: $10.00

All CDs: $15.00

For specific information, please contact:
SOUND & LIGHT MUSIC 800-858-5955

Order by Mail, Website, FAX, or Phone

Quantity	Product	Price
____	_____	$_____
____	_____	$_____
____	_____	$_____

Prices include shipping.
California residents add 7.75% sales tax.

Shipping

Your Name: _____

Church: _____

Address: _____

City/State: _____

Zip: _____Phone: _____

Purchasing

Amount enclosed: $_____

Invoice Church: (p.o.#_____)

VISA/MasterCard: _____–_____–_____–_____

Exp.: _____/_____

Checks payable to: Sound & Light Music
1534 N. Moorpark Rd., Suite #109
Thousand Oaks, CA 91360
FAX 805-497-3152

TOLL FREE! 800-858-5955   **www.IvoryAndBrass.com**